CRISIS OF MORALITY AND REACTION

TO THE HOLOCAUST

JOSEPH REBHUN

BORGO PRESS / WILDSIDE PRESS

www.wildsidepress.com

Copyright © 1998
by Joseph Rebhun

All rights reserved. No part of this book may be reproduced or transmitted in any form or by any means, electronic or mechanical, including photocopying, recording, or any information storage and retrieval system, without permission in writing from the publisher.

Library of Congress Publication Data
Card number: 98-65687
ISBN: 978-1-4344-0364-3

RESURRECTION OF MORALITY

Morality is almost dead and there is an urgent need to revive it if the species Homo sapiens is to continue to exist on the planet earth. The concept of morality is not compatible with the prejudice or intolerance of other races or religions. Prejudice is analogous to phobias, since it is very deeply associated with entrenched perceptions of dangers expected from foreign objects or individuals. The prejudicial fear emotionally sensitizes the individual and encompasses his entire attitude in disregard of contradicting facts. In this book I shall unmask some of the preconceived ideas responsible for the Holocaust, in the hope that this might generally help prevent prejudice, moral nihilism and skepticism.

The mere survival of the human race has become the single, overriding concern of many scientists. With the explosion of the global population and with the means of total destruction, such a cataclysmic event moves from apocalyptic prophecy to a very realistic possibility. The logic of cool and seemingly irreversible timetables, presented by some, is shocking and paralyzing. In order to reverse such a hypothetical end of human civilization, we must effect a total turnabout in our attitudes toward social conditions. Unless this change, combined with a renewed reverence for life, occurs, the not too distant future may bring a holocaust to everyone in spite of the progress of technology and science.

The Holocaust was perpetrated by the Germans, the most educated, technologically advanced, refined and religious people of their era, and was, not so tacitly, approved by the governments of the Christian societies of the West. It took more than one generation and more than one political system to train men capable of cruelties committed by the Nazis. Jack Miles writes in his book, *God, a Biography*[1], that Western civilization is descended equally from Athens and Jerusalem, and he sees a tragedy of God who as Hamlet is trapped-in himself. The death of a people stopped being a tragedy of the dead, but became a tragedy of that civilization that brought this about and is now trapped in its empty morality.

Following the Holocaust, which combined the greatest slaughter and robbery in history with the pinnacle of human criminality, there was little immediate improvement of the Christian attitude to Jews. The total lack of remorse, desecration of Jewish graves, anti-Jewish propaganda in the form of historical revisionism denying the Holocaust, like that by Arthur Butz in the U.S. and by David Irving in England, the vilifying of Judaism as a sinister religion, and using the Talmud in nefarious accusations against the Jews, do not differ from methods used by the Nazis. The physical violence, however, as the pogrom in Kielce, Poland, in 1946, and the more recent bombing of the Jewish community center in Buenos Aires, Argentina, a country which gave asylum to the top Nazi killers with their looted Jewish gold, are the real barometer of the Christian conscience and of the standards of behavior in relation to Jews. This was not a resurgence of anti-Semitism, but the continuation of the old one.

The good news was that both the Catholic and Lutheran Churches admitted their shameful historical role in paving the road to the Holocaust, but they did not work hard enough to disclose their past stand and to remove the old spiritual roots of the anti-Semitic hatred which they had planted so diligently and for so long in the masses of believers. Pope John Paul II condemned the wrong and unjust interpretations of the New Testament, responsible for the lack of spiritual resistance to Nazi persecutions of Jews. He did not, however, direct his criticism to the Roman Catholic Church, the source of those interpretations. It is to his credit that he organized a symposium on the "Roots of Anti-Judaism" and in his Christmas message he hailed Jews for giving Jesus to the world. What a clear contrast it is to the stand of Pius XII.

Not only theologians, but also many lay Church members, who long for morality, are aware of the unjustified Christian prejudice against Jews. Antonin Scalia, the supreme court justice, in his remarks made on May 8, 1997, said: "I am not only not a Jew, but I am a Christian, and I know that the anti-Semitism of many of my uncomprehending co-religionists, over many centuries, helped set the stage for the mad tragedy that the Nazis produced. I say uncomprehending co-religionists, not only because my religion teaches that it is wrong to hate anyone, but because it is particularly absurd for a

Christian to hate the people of Israel. That is to hate one's spiritual parents, and to sever one's roots."

Elie Wiesel wrote me that this manuscript, which was ready almost a quarter century ago, ought to be published. I decided to wait and see if the position of the Christian world with regard to the Holocaust would change. Fortunately it changed for the better. At the time, nuclear weapons were at the center of the conflict between the opponents of the cold war. The sophisticated achievements of the computer age had just started to produce their first fruits in communication, automation and space transportation. In molecular biology, human gene manipulation had not yet become a common practice. The progress of electronic technology, which marked the second half of the 20th century, racing speedily ahead, did not affect the character of man and his morality. Against all expectations, some researchers consider the industriousness and recent inventiveness a paradoxical tool of fate, which might lead to a far more rapid destruction of civilization than that caused by a nuclear war; for example, John Cairns in *Matters of Life and Death*[2]. Ian Wilmut of the Roslin Institute in Scotland, one of the scientists who cloned the sheep Dolly, asked for a ban of human cloning as inhuman. Was there ever a discovery, abandoned by man because it was immoral ? Richard Seed has an answer: "You cannot stop science. It is impossible." He promised to clone man here or abroad.

There are constantly new disclosures of the past dishonesty of western societies. The intention of the Vatican to officially apologize at the end of the millenium for the role the Church played in paving the spiritual road to the Holocaust, does not come from the sudden love for the Jews. It is a response to new historical disclosures which are supposed to serve to strengthen the morality and conscience of the believers. It took over half a century to expose the facts of Nazi collaboration, but it is better late than never. The so called neutral government of Switzerland was a partner with the Nazis, whom it advised how to identify Jews by stamping *J(ude)* on their passports. The heinous behavior during WWII was not limited only to the Swiss bankers. It included their colleagues in Portugal, Spain, Sweden and in other countries. The World Jewish Congress discovered a document that proves gold taken from victims of the Nazis was stored in U.S. and British banks. The polite, "victimized" Austria supplied, proportionally, a greater percentage of the liquidation teams and top echelon Nazis than Germany. Killing masses of Jews with an enthusiasm not smaller than that of the Ukrainians and of the German SS, the Lithuanians would like to have a reputation of another victim of the Nazis. The bishops of France's Roman Catholic Church only recently expressed an apology for their silence, while the Nazis and their French helpers deported French Jews to the annihilation camps. Shortly thereafter followed the apology of the French Order of Doctors for supporting the laws that barred Jewish physicians from practicing. The connivance of the Vichy regime in the "final solution" of French Jewry was known, but now, with the trial of the Nazi collaborators, Klaus Barbie, Paul Touvier and Maurice Papon, it became official. The director of archives for the International Red Cross, George Willemin, explicitly admitted what was known all along, that this organization not only did not help the Jews, but it kept silent while the Nazis starved, tortured and killed six million Jews.

A new moral code, written by Himmler, recommended the killing of the innocent. The Fatherland became the altar for the sacrifice of millions of innocent victims, first legitimizing forced measures in eliminating children born with inborn deficiencies or feeble minded, and then extending this policy to political opponents and to Jews and Gypsies. Good German girls were continuously taught the three K's: Kirche-church, Kinder-children and Kuche-kitchen, and later made their career as SS-women.

Andrei Sakharov, the developer of the hydrogen bomb, examined the dangers inherent in the scientific-technical revolution in a world divided by clashing ideologies. In it he saw the spark of the final catastrophic outcome: a thermonuclear war. He found other perils too: general famine, the pollution of the environment, the evolution of the "mass culture," bureaucratic dogmatism, and cruel demagogy. He perceived a social structure and a psychological orientation, which are the foundations of the totalitarian state.

A police state under a dictatorship, Sakharov says[3], is everywhere involved in a struggle of egoistic and group interests in search of unlimited power and the suppression of intellectual freedom. A police state depends on demagogy, storm trooper tactics, and the propaganda of lies: pure race, Jewish danger, Ukrainophobia, the class struggle, and the cult of personality. The list is endless and the outcome can only be concentration camps, book burning, or the annihilation of an entire people. Intrinsically, a police state has little regard for life. Under conditions such as these, who knows when the control of an atomic arsenal will be in the hands of madmen like a Beria or a Himmler. Thus, this scientist stressed the well-known fact, that the religious tradition exerts an impact on psychological attitudes in interethnic conflicts.

In spite of the end of the cold war and of the disappearance of the pending danger of an immediate nuclear confrontation, nuclear weapons exist and are being sold to fanatics and terrorists. Alexander Lebed, the former Russian general claimed that Russia has lost track of hundred nuclear bombs.

Why is mankind, which can destroy itself many times over, knowingly and blindly going like sheep towards its slaughter? Many ask why the Jews did not take steps to prevent their tragedy, knowing full well that Hitler was serious. Can perhaps these same people offer an analogy with the present situation? People acknowledge the existing perils, but in blind conformity and indifference, do little to prevent them. They are locked into their immediate sphere of interest, losing sight of the large picture, particularly if the moral judgement has to embrace strangers. The relationship of those who are exposed now to the threat of annihilation by the ones in power is certainly more favorable than was the relationship of the Jews to the German totalitarian state.

Many cried out against the injustices of the massacres in Biafra and in My Lai and later on in Rwanda, against the religious wars between the Protestant and Catholic Irish and between Moslem and Christian Yugoslavs. Would the men described by the adjective -fanatical-, a word derived from fanum, a temple, hesitate to burn down the planet in the name of that temple?

New historical discoveries have reawakened interest not only in the Jewish roots of Christianity, but also in the role of the Church in Jewish persecutions ending with the Holocaust, and thus, in a sense, committing matricide. There exists a correlation between the past and present. The persistent anti-Semitism in Poland, in spite of almost a complete absence of Jews in that country, testifies to the fact of how deep religious hatred affects the psyche of the people. Religious prejudice in a Nazi state resulted in the Holocaust. Other totalitarian regimes could use the same techniques of deceit and slaughter, practiced by Hitler, against any ethnic group perhaps under the name of ethnic cleansing. In order to survive, democracy cannot compromise its ideology of individual rights and also be indifferent to occurences beyond its borders. Such an indifference of the West to the impending disaster contributed to the death of the six million Jews in Europe.

Robert Jackson, the American prosecutor at the Nurenberg War Crimes Trials, said : "The wrongs which we seek to condemn and punish have been so calculated, so malignant and so devastating, that civilization cannot tolerate their being ignored because it cannot survive their being repeated."

Worse than indifference and abandonment was a tacit cooperation with the enemy in annihilation of the Jews: refusal to bomb crematoria, as did Roosevelt's advisor, John McCloy, and shutting the entry gates to those Jews who were lucky enough to escape, and delivering them into the hands of the Nazis. Such was the case of the refugees on the ship St. Louis. At the same time the West was profiteering on the loot, which belonged to the victims.

What a state of morality do we find ourselves in, that after more than half a century, the governments of the West, all Christian, caught red-handed, consider the final revelation of those transgressions, magnanimous? Only very recently have we learned about the complicity and cover-up of the West in the Holocaust. Even now, after keeping assets of Jewish martyrs all this time, the banks do not want to release them. The looted Nazi gold was laundered in Canada, Portugal, Argentina, Spain, U.S., other countries, and of course, in Switzerland. Christoph Meili, the Swiss bank guard, who rescued the shredded documents of the Holocaust victims, had to flee his homeland, because of death threats.

The Vatican, which was supposed to be the shining example of Christian ethics, held for safekeeping about 296 million dollars worth of gold plundered from Jews and Serbs by the Croatian Ustache according to a 1946 document of the Treasury Department. The Nazi influence on the Western societies before and during World War II, did not abate after the crimes committed by the Germans became known. Their pervasiveness on social life gave rise to the different shades of the neo-Nazi movements. The real estate left by Jews all over Europe was stolen. I myself could not recover my property in Poland. One hears an outrage caused by the behavior of other countries until news discloses that your own country was not exactly holy. Then, "so what? It was only Jewish gold and the owners were turned into smoke and ashes anyway".

In order to answer questions of morality, such as these, we must go back to the human conduct of the individuals. There is no society which could perform without the cooperation of individuals on whom it is dependent and whom it rules. The example of Denmark and Bulgaria in WWII is a confirmation of the fact that, if there are enough people in a society, who are willing to take a stand, even under totalitarianism, such as that of the Nazis, disobedience and defense of freedom is possible. For resistance such as this, people need a highly ethical climate capable of repelling the most subtle or violent of human rights violations. Individuals with high moral conscience form such a social climate. Under the Nazis the majority of the Germans, to use Eichmann's own words, were "nothing but a tiny screw in a gigantic machine," and as losers of their individual morals and ethics, they became murderous robots. On the other hand, the small number of Christians, who in spite of prevailing pressures and personal danger, helped the condemned Jews, became apostles of love. They will remain in the annals of mankind in clear contrast to the criminals who helped the Nazis, or rejoiced at the *Final Solution,* of their neighbors and friends. At a discussion of the Polish-Jewish relations, organized by the American Jewish Committee, a Polish representative asked why the Jews criticize the Poles more than others for their anti-Semitism, especially during the Nazi time, since the Poles did not behave worse than others. He was right for posing this question. The Jews considered themselves brothers and expected more from the Poles, from whom only the Catholic religion separated them.

The question arises as to why Christianity, being the daughter religion of Judaism, felt as it did about the Jews? Was this hatred based only on myths and superstitions of the Christians about the Jews?

There are basic philosophical differences in religious attitude between Judaism and Christianity:

The *receiving* salvation of the Christians by professing in Jesus, who died for one's sins, against the Jewish idea of individual responsibility and justice, *giving*, as the guiding yardstick of righteousness. The extension of this basic philosophy of Judaism is tolerance and love for the stranger (non-Jew), which precedes in order even the love for orphans and widows. This tolerance also differentiates Judaism from any other philosophical system showing intolerance, for example, the one professed by Louis Farrakhan in this country, or by Jean-Marie Le Pen in France. The merits of the believer are judged by his own deeds, *maasim tovim*, here and now, and there is very little talk in Judaism about the hereafter. The role of God is described in Judaism as that of the Creator and the final Arbiter. All the anthropomorphic attributes, the different personalities ascribed to God by Jack Miles, even if they are naively found in the Bible, are not Jewish. A Jew cannot describe his God in any other way, only that He exists: *El HAI V'KAJAM*, and His orders are clear and brief, as in the words of Micah: "What does the Lord require of you, but to do justly, to love mercy, and to walk humbly with your God." Life is holy. The Jews, even aside from their religion, believe that each man is a universe unto himself, and that individual freedom and rights should be guaranteed by society. This is the paramount lesson mankind should learn from the Holocaust, if it wishes to survive.

There was a fundamental socio-philosophical background to the Jewish catastrophe during World War II. It was based on the clash between liberal individualism with its emphasis on moral conscience, and the surging totalitarian ideas which transform man into a mechanical robot. One had to make a definite decision: would he preserve his own integrity, even at the risk of his life, or would he try to become absorbed by the mass psychosis? It has become obvious that a totalitarian regime may easily perpetrate crimes against individuals and groups without fear of resistance. We must remember the Roman saying: *hodie mihi, cras tibi*, (today it happened to me, tomorrow it might happen to you) and to learn from the past, in order to avoid an historical replay. The rules of totalitarianism are the same, though the victims may vary. The catastrophe that befell the Jews was not just an isolated, unfortunate crime of a diabolically inhuman system. It is a portent of what might happen to us all.

Unfortunately, past history cannot be altered. A lesson, however, may be drawn from it. It is time that man learns tolerance and love for others, the basis of not only Jewish belief, but of morality in general. Should he continue to be a piece of mechanism, or share with others a religious or philosophical system without an individual conscience, no matter who the immediate victims may be, mankind will eventually blow itself off the surface of the earth. Only by a drastic change in man's attitude can another holocaust be averted. At the same time, and more subtly, by the dehumanizing of mass culture, by arresting individual conscience and unleashing the incalculable destructive powers of a sophisticated technological system, it can slowly become the greatest danger even to all of mankind. The Nazi Holocaust was exactly this.

It is necessary to clarify a number of popular misconceptions. First, Jews are not a race. Persecutions of Jews should be called anti-Judaism, and not anti-Semitism. Judeo-Christian culture is also a misnomer, because of the predominating element of symbology and imagery of the Greek and Roman religions in Christianity. During the Roman Empire, at the time of Jesus, Judaism was the religion doing the most proselytizing, and there were about three times as many Jews living outside of Palestine as in their own country. In the Middle Ages, forced conversions brought hundreds of thousands of Jews into the ranks of the Christian Church joined later by numbers of those who trickled in voluntarily. One does not know, therefore, if the number of the descendants of the original Hebrews is not greater among the Christians than among today's Jews. It would be ironical if Jewish grandchildren in Nazi uniforms killed the grandchildren of the citizens of the Roman Empire who accepted Judaism. For example, a Mr. B., an engineer from Hamburg, told me that during the war he was an intelligence officer for the Gestapo. His Catholic family was recently shocked after it traced its origin to a converted chief rabbi of Frankfurt in 1820.

The persecution of the Jews was not directed against them as individuals but rather against the religious ideas of Judaism. It is common knowledge that present-day Christianity differs from the Church of Jesus which in his lifetime consisted entirely of Jews. Powell Davies presents very succinctly in his book, *The Meaning of the Dead Sea Scrolls,*[4] the difference between the *historical* Christianity founded by Jesus and the one practiced since the encroachment of paganism. He claims that scholars have known this difference throughout history, but not so the laymen. Furthermore, Davies sees the adaptation of the pagan teaching about Mithras by Christianity to be so important that he perceives the possibility of the existence of the new church even without the person of Jesus. According to Mathew, Jesus said: "Don't think that I have come, to abolish the Torah or the Prophets. I have come not to abolish, but to complete." We read, also in Mathew, that Jesus was a believing Jew, not a Christian, and was teaching his followers: " Worship Adonai your God, and serve only Him". Christianity however fought the Torah by sword and fire even from its earliest beginnings. Another teaching of Jesus, that the Christians have forgotten, is: "You have heard that our fathers were told 'love your neighbor and hate your enemy.' But I tell you: love your enemies! Pray for those, who persecute you" (Mathew 5). Like the Prophets before Him, Jesus was against sacrifices: "I want compassion rather than animal sacrifices".

The Jewish community was for centuries approached by proselytizing Christian missionaries. According to the Los Angeles Times (August 9, 1997), Robert L. Carneiro of the Museum of Natural History in New York said that, through the centuries, missionaries have killed nonbelievers, kidnapped natives, enslaved populations, separated children from parents, banned languages and annihilated traditions. "Missionary work is theological imperialism," he said. All those methods and worse were practiced with Jews. Even now, after the Holocaust and historical, theological revisionism within Christianity, there is a very intense effort of evangelists to convert Jews. They still now offer redemption to a people who brought mankind the Ten Commandments. A Jew, brainwashed by such an evangelist, was asked: "What will you do, when Jesus will come back?" "I will shake hands with Him, because He will come as an orthodox Jew. But what will *you* do? If you like to be a Christian, be a Christian. Judaism was good enough for Jesus, so it is good enough for me," answered the Jew. In real life such a discussion in an intolerant environment with a brawling, fear-preaching evangelist might provoke a physical response.

By far the most important reason for the persecution of the Jews was the hatred cultivated by eighteen centuries of Church teachings, a congenital malady of the Christians, propagated by those who were supposed to represent on earth the authority of the great Healer who died on the Cross. Hate instilled by saints and popes became a mystic force, especially when combined with the teachings of deicide. Gradually there developed the Christian myth of the Jew-Satan; malicious and powerful, capable even of killing the Son of God, representing all that is reprehensible. The stereotyped picture of the Jew painted by the Church Fathers drew all the wrath of the believers at their times of crisis and misfortune.

The masses of believers were and still are barred from the historical truth, and the teaching of deicide became the basis of the traditional Christian religion, and in the words of Frank Eiklor, many sermons "sound like the very belching of hell." This noble Christian calls anti-Semitism: the scandal of the Church history. This history, fed to the believers, was distorted and based on fabrications. Even when the unbelievers rejected dogma, the inherited object of hate was retained. There are two reasons for this: it is hard to break with a long tradition, and it is psychologically more convenient to blame somebody else, for one's misfortune and lack of success. Those Christians who rejected the Church's dogma were even more unhappy and concentrated on the second feeling, hatred of the Jews. There were many of them, from Martin Luther to Hitler. In order for both, individuals and groups to preserve their psychological "balance," the loss of the Church's support was compensated by a more intense expression of hatred. The universal love preached by the Jew-God Jesus and the hatred of his brother, Jew-Satan, was the greatest contradiction of the Christian Church and resulted in ages of persecution of Jews and attempts at their annihilation. Today's anti-Semites, racists, neo-Nazis, skinheads and bigots of different coloring, are mostly non-believers, and so are the intellectuals who deny the existence of the Holocaust, for example Professor Butz from Northwestern University and those who have now found on the Internet a convenient medium to spread their lies. But there are many evil believers, who know the truth and are lying about the Holocaust; for example Pat Buchanan, who denied that Jews suffered in the Holocaust and that they were killed in Treblinka by diesel-engine gas and later on by Zyklon- B gas.

There are changes in theological ideas, both among Christians and Jews, mainly concerned with God's role in the life of man. A young Jewish man was raised during and after the Holocaust by a Polish Catholic woman, whom he called–mother. He told me, that after she said good bye to him before his departure for the United States, she added: "there is no God in heaven, if such things as the Holocaust could have happened." The role of God during the Holocaust, as the defender of the faithful, the merciful Father, the shield of Abraham, was not seen by some Jews. It is obvious, they say, that God did not protect the six million Jews, which means that He either does not exist, doesn't interfere in human affairs, or worse - He does not care. This introduced a third step in the evolution of Jewish theology: first, Abraham rejected human sacrifices, then, the prophets recognized no need for animal sacrifices, replacing them by social justice, and finally, the Holocaust did not see God's intervention in human affairs, retaining only His role of the Creator and the Master of the universe.

On the other hand, the Jews ask, what kind of God did the enemies of the Jews have, a God who helped the killers? In their conception, theological dreams are but myths without morality.

Fortunately, Judaism possesses other values, which are essential for its preservation: it is an *ethical* monotheism. The Jew was commanded only to "walk humbly with his God" and not necessarily expect something in return. He believed in the sanctity of life, love for other members of his species, and in absolute justice in inter-human relations. Good deeds could bring man spiritual salvation in this life. The hereafter, if it exists, is unknown. Rabbi Jacob said in *Ethics of The Fathers* "Better is one hour of repentance and of good deeds in this world than the whole life of the world to come."

Christians' believes concentrate on the hereafter, on a belief in hell from which God can save man, only if he believes in Jesus Christ. Without this belief all the good deeds will not save man from eternal damnation.

In spite of the great evangelical promotion of Christianity by different churches, there is a crisis at the highest intellectual level, starting from atheists, like Don Cupitt *"After God, the Future of*

Religion," or a former Roman Catholic priest, John Dominic Crossan *"Who Killed Jesus,"* following the entire gamut of theologians, who see in Jesus a historical figure, deprived of any divine aspects. They believe that Jesus was a person, who was not raised from the dead, which is a basic Christian doctrine (Newsweek, April 8,1996 *Rethinking the Resurrection*). While some scholars call for replacement of the "cultic" with the historical, "real" Jesus, the average Christian doesn't care about the historical Jesus. He will continue to believe in the traditional one.

More laymen, who become more sophisticated and reject dogmas, ask for scientific truth and logical reasons for the inhuman hate of Jews implanted into the hearts of believers by the Church. When heaven and earth seek an explanation for the death of a people, the Church must answer, if not for the sake of the perished and of the truth, then for its own preservation. There has to appear some objective decency. The blood bath of the Holocaust was so overwhelming that, with the annihilation of six million innocent lives, it practically drowned the justifications of Christian ethics and logic. The current ecumenical movement is an attempt to retard the downfall of Christian morality. It is the first ray of a new feeling of guilt for the false teachings and indifference to the fate of an innocent people. But even now there are conservatives in the Church who would like to still the wakening conscience of the Christians. They fight ecumenism, and they try to sweep away the mounting historical evidence of the true Jewish origin of Christianity. These conservatives would rather not listen to the truth about the six million and the many more millions who were put to death before. Fortunately, they are in the minority. The majority, particularly in the democratic countries, primarily in the United States, seeks a genuine dialogue with the Jews.

In the eyes of some Jews, the Christians do not deserve a dialogue. Dagobert D. Runes is one of these. In his book, *The Jew and the Cross*[5] he outlined his feelings and urged that a papal edict make it clear that the Jews are and were not guilty of deicide.

I feel that without such an acquittal of the "Big Sin" there is no future for mankind. As I shall elaborate further on, I do not forgive or forget, but I feel that there is a way of atonement; and in order to show Christians the way we must enter into a dialogue with them. Indeed, it is our human obligation to sustain it until the redemption is reached, till the Church not only professes the truth, but corrects that which is still correctable. One way of redemption is for the Church to reverse itself loudly and to admit that it persecuted the Jews unjustly. It must acknowledge that it falsely indoctrinated its believers for centuries about Jewish crimes never committed, and that it was a tacit and indifferent bystander when the smoky souls of Jewish children were flying out of the chimneys of Auschwitz.

Though this historical breather in Jewish martyrdom came much too late, we have to use it as long as our interlocutor will stick to historical truth and justice. Both sides have the opportunity to present their cases. This dialogue cannot be a "tournament for God and truth" between rabbis and priests. Not many people know historical facts. Most people believe what they are told. It is up to the organized clergy, responsible in the past for spreading false ideas, to disseminate the historical truth. One has to observe with satisfaction that a great number of Catholic clergymen, especially the young ones, understood John XXIII's call never to distort the truth.

Jews cannot slam the door on the Christian world no matter how much they suffered in it. They have to continue to live in that world and have to establish a *modus vivendi*. They must also retain the moral obligation to help others see the light of human brotherhood, even, if some of the non-Jews are guilty of the greatest crimes. If we should lose the idea of redemption for mankind, we would lose hope for a better future. Opening the road of redemption to the sinners does not mean to forgive, but to give a chance for the psychological debt of mankind to balance out. We can not and should not close the past and put the Holocaust behind us. Christianity has to live forever with the crime and guilt for paving the spiritual road for the Holocaust. We should be glad that the Church has made an attempt at dialogue. This might be the first step of enlightenment coming from within the hierarchy, the only way Christianity can go back to the teachings of Jesus and reject paganism with the monstrous demonism created by the Church Fathers. The revolution coming from the laymen, however, rather than from the organized Church, no matter how educated they are, and how clearly they recognize past superstitions and fabrications of the Church, would probably retain the inbred atavistic hate for Jews *a la* Martin Luther. Only by following the real teachings of Jesus can the Church create a spiritual atmosphere for a Judeo-Christian civilization, which now is only a meaningless word, a figment of imagination.

On the other hand, intelligent, truth-seeking Christian laity will exert a pressure on the conservative circles of the hierarchy to reveal the true history and blot out lies and distortions from teachings about the highest human values. The closer the Church gets to logic and truth, the closer its teaching will be to Jesus, the Jew, and to his love of Jews. It will also get further from the hatred rooted in centuries and planted by the saints, who contradicted their Master.

A sincere attempt to tell the story of Jewish persecutions is made by Edward H. Flannery[6], a Catholic priest. If only his book became obligatory reading for every Christian, the Church would not utter such words as "perfidious Jews" and "Christ Killers" anymore. Evaluating the Greek and Roman discrimination against Jews, Flannery[6] sees the roots of the Christian persecutions to come. Once singled out by their ancient enemies, the Jews, according to the author, became victims of an historical snowballing process of prejudicial treatment. He admits that the Greco-Roman attitude was a reaction against Jewish separatism and defiance of the aggressive forces of imperialism. It was not "eternal" or permanent; it was not dictated by racial bias, political reasons or prevailing economic factors; it seldom was an expression of the masses, but rather of a handful of writers. Father Flannery should continue his comparison with the Christian attitude—which he does not.

Christianity added to this undesirable, but existing, prejudicial relationship between Jews and non-Jews, religious hatred based on deicide. While rational motives in interpersonal and international relations can always find an explanation, this relationship between men who were told to be killers of God and of the cosmos became irrational, not disputable, eternal, irreparable in its absurdity. It was based on the impossibility of killing the One that by its definition is eternal and cannot be killed. Based on such a belief, Christians exercised their revenge on those who "killed" their God, considering the act of persecution and killing Jews a cooperative venture with the absolute goodness,

God Himself.

From this poison root grew the weeds of hate which took over the souls of believers and was developed as an integral part of the Christian doctrine. Here was the seedbed of the stereotype of the Jew as fixed in the minds of the Gentiles and as portrayed in their literature. Even after their annihilation or expulsion from a country, the Jews remained the objects of hatred and mockery, as they are now in Poland, and as they were at the time of Shakespeare's writing *The Merchant of Venice*, in England. The Jew, once condemned by the Church Fathers, was displayed with attributes of wickedness and seen as Satan. As Christian character degenerated the Jew was the object of even greater persecution.

The Christian person learned to project his own transgressions on this stereotype. He was afraid of Jesus, the source of his ethical standards and the judge of all sinners. This fear of punishment and eternal hell became the obsessive idea of the Christian who, in his search for salvation, found it necessary to unload his responsibility and condemnation on somebody else. The source of his threat through Jesus, a Jew, was eventually identified with the source of the wickedness, the Satan-Jew.

Thus, the Christian found an outlet for three of his psychological needs: he was buying God's favors for punishing the anti-God; he was unloading his ballast of sin on the Jew, thereby ridding himself of the guilt; and he was finding an easy way of getting even with the source of his eternal threat.

Such psychological gains were topped off with other gratification, which in later centuries became more dominant: satisfaction of sadistic impulses and avidity, greediness, and incentives toward achievements and treasure hunting. The existence of the stereotype Jew was psychologically useful for filling in almost any lacking explanation, any intellectual void, and in providing the foundations of gossip and legends.

Christian writers of the early centuries invented the original stories of Jewish violence against Christians, and since they burned Jewish books at the same time, the only source of this accusation was the plaintiff himself. He achieved what he sought: the exposure of defenseless Jews to almost two millennia of a kangaroo court finally adjourned in Auschwitz.

The wicked offensive against Judaism, pointing out that the Church is the true Israel, antedating Jews, could not foresee that long after Jewish historical sources were destroyed, the Dead Sea Scrolls would reveal that the first Christians represented only one of several Jewish sects and, as such, was not an original religion.

The past stand was not always clear: when it suited the writer, he expressed his envy for the Jews, the "chosen people." At other times the Church became the "chosen people" and the tone of the writer about Jews became derogatory.

These attitudes of envy and ridicule persisted till Goebbels and Trophim Kichko's *Judaism Without Embellishment.*[7]

St. Justin's idea that the Jews were deserving of punishment became a green light for all those who wanted to help God do a good job-including Hitler. The circulated Testimonies, the teachings of Hippolitus and Chrysostom's *"Adversus Judaeos"*[8] became the prototype of the *"Protocols of the Elders of Zion"*. Christian theologians worked less feverishly than their Nazi students; they just laid the foundations for the monumental tragedy of the Final Solution. Jews could not defend themselves in a free theological dispute. The Church Fathers were afraid of free expression and often resorted to physical terror against the Jews. Chrysostom's formulation of the deicidal theory, spliced with all the other vicious attributes he pinned on the Jew, plus the teachings of Martin Luther, together with *Mein Kampf*, resulted in the twentieth century's virulent anti-Judaism. Under suitable conditions, a proper stimulus could evoke a murderous reflex.

Why did the Church Fathers prepare this inhuman suffering for the Jews? Many answers were offered. The Church was a heretical new institution whose teachings had to combat the mother religion—as any new system tries to fight the established one: it competed with Judaism for the souls of the pagans, and finally, the takeover by the Church of the powers of Constantine's empire brought masses of pagans into the Church. Those pagans in turn influenced the Church, which by that time had already accepted Jesus' deity. This new symbiosis could not tolerate the Jewish element in its philosophy.

In spite of certain anthropomorphic features, by which Jewish Scriptures describe God, He was always considered "to have neither a bodily form nor substance and no man can compare to Him in His holiness." The apotheosis of Jesus, a man, could not be accepted. This was not the first time the Jews were ready to suffer for rejecting the cult of a person. Both the rejection of this cult combined with the preservation of individual freedom of belief and the inability to transplant Jewish teachings preached by Jesus into the pagan society were the basic reasons for the clash of Judaism and Christianity. This is not to mention contradictory teachings of Christianity.

The transplant of Jewish ideas can be compared to a graft rejection: during the first generation of Christians it seemed to "take." Later, the body of the pagan world formed antibodies, and the transplant was finally destroyed during the Hitler era.

The forceful methods used by the Church started with the building of an ideological framework for the Christian theology, which forced an extreme polarization of the two religions.

Violent imposition and intolerance replaced the free competition of theological ideas as soon as the Church grasped state power. By attaining this instrument of force and using it unjustly, the Church differed from other heretic branches of Judaism such as the Karaites, who, though remaining in opposition to the mother religion, did not turn matricidal. The theological anti-Judaism of Christianity did not hesitate to silence the opposing arguments and often, those who uttered them, forever. The ideas of deicide and of the divine punishment of the Jews became imprinted in Christian minds more than did the believer's personal salvation.

Jules Isaac dwells on the Church's original accusations of Jews in his book, *The Teaching of Contempt*[9]. This teaching, repeated daily for eighteen centuries, forced its way even into the minds of critical, supposedly objective historians. The power of false propaganda can become so strong that it can rival truth even in those who, by virtue of their profession, should be more critical than others. For example, Catholic teachings that the dispersion of the Jews is a punishment for the Crucifixion is historically false. The Diaspora existed long before Jesus and before destruction of the Temple in

70 A.D. And yet contemporary historians repeat the lie of the third and fourth century theologians that 70 A.D. is the beginning of the dispersion. Why is this fabrication not condemned and corrected? Another fabrication of the Church Fathers, which now hangs as a shameless red herring on the historical scaffold is the contention that the religion of the Jews in the time of Jesus was a legalistic institution without a soul. Isaac points to the spiritual life that existed among Jewish sects at the time of Jesus as seen in the description of the Essenes in the Dead Sea Scrolls. Christianity was born from those sects and remained essentially Jewish before the influx of pagan doctrines. Isaac exposes the big lie of Chrysostom , which became the pivotal idea of deicide in Christian theology. Jesus professed the belief in one God (Mark 12: 28-29). He considered himself a Jew and was crucified by the Romans as were many other Jews. Crucifixion was not a method of killing by Jewish law. It was a device of Roman invention. Even if stretching the responsibility for the death of Jesus on those who were close to the Romans would draw animosity against the influential Jews, the mass of Jews are described in the Gospel as mourning the crucified, innocent Teacher. Those Jews who knew Jesus did not know that he would be considered a Messiah. He called himself the "Son of Man" and imposed on his disciples the upholding of the secrecy that he was the Christ (Matthew 16:20). How could the other Jews know and accept his uncommon nature if he himself forbade anyone to reveal it? Until the second century Jesus was called the Messiah or the Son of Man. The epithet "Son of God" or "God" was added later by converted Greeks. Furthermore only a small number of the Jews ever met him or heard about him. The majority of them lived outside the country and could by no stretch of the imagination be responsible for the death of their brother, Jesus, whom they did not even know. As for the Romans, they were guilty of homicide, not of deicide. They would never bother about an innocent Messiah. They wanted only to get rid of a possible political troublemaker whom they mocked as *rex Judaeorum*. Peter accused the Jews of Jerusalem of exactly this: of homicide through their ignorance of who Jesus really was. This was a false accusation ascribed to Peter and created by the pen of the non-contemporary Gospel writers. The greater the inroads of Christianity in the pagan world, says Isaac, the more the Romans were excused and the Jews accused.

Jaroslav Pelican stresses in his book, *Jesus Through the Centuries,* not only the human nature of Jesus, but the fact that He was a Jew, and his teachings were purely Jewish. Between the lines one reads his accusation the Christians of hatred, persecution and displays of anti-Semitism directed against the Jews.

There is a similarity in the means and methods used in persecutions of Jews by the Church and by the totalitarian dictatorships, particularly that of Nazi Germany. Although many recognize the absolute control of ideas by the Church in the past to the degree that any deviation or free thinking was anathema, only a few have spelled out the common general characteristics between the two.

According to Friedrich and Brzezinski[10], the totalitarian dictatorships have an official ideology dominating all aspects of life and destined to rule the world. Other characteristics are the hierarchy of activists led by one man and controlling, through one party and bureaucratic organization, the full implementation of the ideology; police and secret service as the party's instrument of terror. The party has a monopoly of control over all mass communications media for the proliferation of propaganda. Such a monopoly of control by the party also extends over the armed forces and economic life.

The first two characteristics apply to the Church. However, the authors do not suggest the identification of the Catholic Church with totalitarian dictatorship. For example, there is a doctrinal ideology binding the Church followers with the hierarchical leadership. The elections of the pope by the College of Cardinals, and of the leader in a totalitarian dictatorship are similar. As the party's activists legitimize the absolutism of the dictator by their choice, the cardinals bestow the right of infallibility on the pope. This procedure by the totalitarian dictatorship and the Church is a part of the ideology and power structure of both systems and is supported by the orthodox activists.

The idea of expansion and conquest by force or conversion existed in the Church long before the modern totalitarian states came into existence. The conversion of the masses is now facilitated in totalitarian states by the monopoly control of the communications media. Previously, the ideology of the Church was spread from every pulpit and through every other aspect of missionary work.

Any method was good, whether it was through teaching human love and salvation, or through bloody conquest.

The totalitarian states criticize, reject, and combat the preexistent systems much as the Church did with Judaism. They use arguments-dogmas, whether logical or not, based less on truth than on myths. These basic "truths" are convictional and indisputable. They cannot be reasoned or understood, and they must be accepted. Magic and prejudice take the place of reason and logic, and when necessary, are made acceptable by absolute force. The emotional myths, and not rational factors, are premises for tactics of a system as, for example, in the development of the doctrine of deicide, or of the Nazi race theory.

The attitudes toward life and the methods expressing this relationship show great similarities between the Church and modern totalitarian systems. These similarities are even greater in relation to the fictitious enemy. Though totalitarian systems (Church and state) were combating each other, they had the same stereotyped enemy created in the fourth century by the Church fathers. In order to picture this enemy in the worst light, myths, lies, and forgeries were presented as a part of the official ideology and holy doctrine supported by the powerful authority of the system. Both Church and state could achieve an easy victory with a non-belligerent enemy and finally show that they were inevitably successful. In order to achieve a psychological balance in the masses of followers for the unjustified persecutions and terrorizing of the Jews, both the Church and the totalitarian state create their own martyrs, heroes, holy men, and saints.

To equalize the guilt for the overwhelming crimes perpetrated on Jews, each system (Church and totalitarian state) ascribes to the Jew omnipotent, ubiquitous, and apocalyptic attributes. This fraud becomes not only a part of the propaganda but also a religious and ideological credo enforced by terror. The more illogical the dogma, the more violence is necessarily applied by the totalitarian system to implement it, and the more blind submission is expected from party members and church hierarchy in spreading the gospel. The teaching of hate for the "enemies of the people" and "God killers" is emphasized more than the teaching of love.

Thus, in addition to the hate cultivated by the Church for centuries, the modern totalitarian state adopted similar methods to the Jewish question and, availing itself of the new technology, expanded the propaganda and killing to macabre proportions. Outright forgeries like the *Protocols of the Elders of Zion* were viciously disseminated by party and state authority and believed by the masses. I disagree with Hannah Arendt[11], who differentiates the modern anti-Christian anti-Judaism from the old religious Jew hatred. Though some Christians became anti-Christian under Nazism and Bolshevism, the Jew, the object of their hatred, did not change. The psychological basis of modern anti-Judaism has been found to be formed by the emotional attitudes transferred by tradition and imbibed with the mother's milk. Hate lasts longer than love in those who are possessed by both emotions: with the decline of positive Christian values, therefore, the hate toward Jews does not lessen in intensity. Anti-Judaism is a dormant, latent sickness, likely to reappear at any time.

In addition to this most important historical factor of singling out the Jew for hatred by the organized Christian religion, other elements helped to mold the anti-Jewish attitude. The Jews, who, more than others, follow liberal ideas, were endowed with the blessings of European liberalism. Pulzer[12] studied the link between Jewish history and that of liberal thought.

At first, modern anti-Judaism involved only the conservative, politically dominant, groups of the society, which turned against liberalism. But after decades of hammering propaganda it also engulfed the masses. The blindness of the people caused them to turn against the freedoms created by liberal politics, though the masses were the ones to benefit from them the most. The mystic hate prevailed over rational tolerance.

With the diminishing role of the Church in the age of liberalism, the newer anti-Jewish attitude lacked spiritual authority. In order to create a new apocalyptic mystification behind the hate facade and to give it a broader psychological base, the theory of racial superiority was developed. The writings of Mann, Fritsch, Duhring, Chamberlain, and many others were full of fantastic lies and distortions and became a powerful source for Nazi propaganda. Some presented Jesus as an Aryan and anti-Semite; others turned away from Jesus and the Old Testament as Jewish by-products and returned to paganism. In the renaissance of Germanic prehistory paganism and blood theory matured into Nazi racial "mysticism." The Germans would dominate the world only after the elimination of the threatening Jewish genius and its inferior blood.

The Jewish racial instinct, claimed the Germans, leads to sexual promiscuity. This accusation was expressed to me personally by a prominent lay Catholic in Hamburg in 1968. He was surprised when I told him that the sex offense is one of the greatest sins, that according to Jewish law, adultery, idolatry, and murder should not be committed even under the threat of death. Chastity was stressed in Jewish education more than anything else. Prostitution was forbidden among Jews. Historically, the sexual isolation of Jews from non-Jews was meant to protect the national culture, purity, and sanctity of the family from the influence of the cults of Baal, Astarte, and Dionysus. If there is any violation of the seventh and tenth commandments by a Jew, it is relatively rare. This mature, intelligent German was so brain washed that he had never bothered to examine charges such as these and believed naively that the Talmud orders Jews to perform acts of sexual promiscuity and perversion offending non-Jewish partners.

Summing up: with the anti-Jewish fabrications, the race theory, the sex criminality, and the degenerative potential to undermine German sanity, Nazism created fundamental anti-Jewish anxiety originating not only from the old apocalyptic crime of deicide, but from the more immediate danger to one's blood and health. A part of such anti-Jewish sentiments might stem from Christianity's undeniable Jewish heritage in a people committed to complete racial purity. The hatred of the Jews became a means whereby they might rid themselves of elements of that heritage which they considered foreign. This resulted in self-hatred, which is akin to the "child battering syndrome" of demented parents.

The unique character of the Jews, who were a "nation among nations" and preserved their different religion, customs, and values, though they considered themselves German nationals, often more patriotic than the non-Jewish Germans, is contradictory to this system of pure race, personality cult, and totalitarian philosophy. A personality cult is incompatible with Judaism and totalitarianism itself is anti-Judaism, even without discrimination against the Jews. The collective Jewish identity was religious, cultural, traditional, historical, but not racial. Although the Bible forbade intermarriage (Deuteronomy 7:1-3), this law was widely broken at different times: before Ezra, during hellenization, in the time of Roman hegemony, during decades of liberalism, etc. In addition, Jewish women were more exposed to the rape of the invading armies than others because of their geographical dispersion. The Jews knew that neither they nor any other people were racially pure and therefore considered all racial theories as fabrications (the same as the idea of deicide) useful as justifications for persecuting the innocent.

Any Jew, besides having Jewish parents, had a free choice whether to retain Judaism or not. The environment of the host nation affected many to the point that they chose to reject Judaism and to accept Christianity. Nazis considered those first, second, and third generation Christians as Jews who had to be deported to the crematoria. Baptism could save them from the "guilt" of deicide but not from the supposed impurity of racial characteristics. This should be clear to today's "Jews for Jesus" and to the Messianic Judaism, supported by the fundamentalist Christians as a religious fifth column, to convert Jews to Christianity.

Church law was satisfied with destroying the spirit of Judaism; the Nuremberg Law and the Final Solution asked for Jewish blood and the extermination of the Jewish *race*. Without the precedent of the Canonic law, abrogating Jewish rights, the Nuremberg laws could not exist in a truly Christian society.

The Catholic Church, as well as the Nazi regime, used unfounded generalizations as the mode of false accusations of the Jews: *all* Jews are *always* guilty of deicide; *all* Jews everywhere are crooks and typhus carriers, and for their perversity they must inevitably receive God's punishment. The Jew in a western metropolis or in an eastern village, though far apart, was considered a member of an international conspiracy. This organized body of Jews, striving for world domination, used capital or secret power to rule capitalist or communist governments.

There was no possibility of individual virtue or merit that could break this general rule. The Jews had no chance to present an historical proof of their innocence. Church authorities burned Jewish books before the Nazis did.

No matter what good qualities Jews might have, they could not cancel out the greatest crime of all—to be born Jewish. For the Germans, the foregoing statement was a contradiction in itself since a Jew is all criminality and cannot possibly have any good attributes. Accordingly, there were laws directed against all Jews. The Church paved the way to Nuremberg. Raul Hilberg[13] showed this in a table form: the canonical laws are reflected in their Nazi anti-Jewish measures. These laws had provisions for the Jews to pay for the crimes committed against them; Jews had to compensate Christian missionaries for converting them to Christianity and had to pay for the Nazi crimes of the "Crystal Night." There is also a generalization in reverse: the Jews are enemies and tormenters of Christianity; they are a danger to all Germany. The same highly charged emotional attitude may be found in Martin Luther's book, *About the Jews and Their Lies*[14]. One would have hoped that after he broke with Rome, he would revise his existing stand toward the Jews. Instead, his vicious writings became an introductory source for the ideas of Goebbels and Streicher. The psychological impact of Martin Luther on the Germans was so great that he alone is considered by some to be the spiritual father of Hitlerism. This will be the subject of discussion in my next chapter.

Chapter 2.

SALVATION AND SACRIFICE

The smokescreen of imagined inherent Jewish racial criminality affected even those who themselves were victims of totalitarianism, such as Poles and Lithuanians. It was responsible for their hostile posture, for the delivering of those Jews, who ran for their lives or assumed Aryan identity, into the hands of the Gestapo, for the brutal killing of Jewish partisans in the forests by the Polish "Armja Krajowa," Land army, and, at best, for the apathy toward their suffering. This was also the reason why hundreds of Jewish survivors of concentration camps were killed in Poland upon their return to their homeland after the war. It is putative that one political system and one generation could create so much evil.

The "all or none" attitude toward the Jews shared by the Church as well as by the Germans became part of their religious belief, combined with the idea of salvation. This religious stand in politics blinded the Germans completely.

After they had pillaged all Jewish property and fully exploited Jewish slave labor for war production, the Nazis still went into debt, losing three billion Reichsmarks worth of labor plus costly transportation of their victims and the cost of manpower used in extermination of Jews. Was it insanity or obsession on the part of the *Herrenvolk*? How could an otherwise intelligent people with some degree of excellence in science and medicine, warfare and politics, philosophy and literature develop such a brutal system of "racial" annihilation?

To both the Church and the Nazis, the focal idea of their belief was salvation, which could be achieved only through an outside factor, whether it was the atonement of Jesus, or the victory of the party. Jews attain salvation on the basis of their own merits plus God's grace. Since the party's victory was expected right here on earth and not in heaven, the goal of the Nazis was to be achieved through the eradication of the fictitious enemy, the Jew. Such an attitude was unquestionably expressed in the official newspaper of the Nazi party, the *Voelkischer Beobachter*, on May 24, 1934. The ideology of National Socialism which strengthened the Germans by emphasizing the nationalist nature of politics influenced not only Germans living abroad, but also foreign nations. It brought a new concept into political thinking on the nature of the state and, for Germans, an easing of their difficult struggle for salvation. Who was the savior to rescue the Germans? For them it was Hitler. Thus, the Church and the Nazis both subscribed to a crude, primitive philosophy of salvation as an undeserved gift for which they paid by offering the same human sacrifice-the Jews. Both systems were afraid they would lose ground if they declared that the enemy was fictional and his guilt nonexistent. Should the theologians of the twentieth century not be superior to their predecessors of the fourth century and have the courage to replace lies about the Jews with the truth? Should they not finally realize that the Creator does not need human sacrifices to bring mankind salvation? Abraham, the first Jew, discovered this out on Mount Moriah almost four thousand years ago!

The Church did not succeed in converting the Jews to Christianity either by force—by means of the Crusades, the auto-da-fe, the Inquisition—or by persuasion. A few left the ranks only after unbearable and unrelenting terror. There are such basic differences between Judaism and Christianity that the two could not possibly amalgamate.

And yet the anti-Jewish philosophy never aimed at complete annihilation of the "older brother." This was because of the role the Church purported to play by upholding ethical standards and the theory of the "Witness-People." This theory, created by St.Augustine, claimed that Christianity needs a living witness to its truth. By their suffering and misfortune the Jews prove that the Christian God condemns those who do not accept Him and the new religion.

Pope Innocent III embraced this idea as well as the idea of deicide, giving Christians the blessing of infallibility presented to the Fourth Lateran Council. The canons of that Council became the prototype of the Nuremberg Code. A new Church tactic affecting Jews became law: an external distinction separating them from others manifested itself outwardly in a particular manner of dress, which became, in our time, the yellow badge of the ghetto.

Centuries of this treatment conditioned the Jews to accept it as a way of life. Since the "Witness-People" were condemned, they were permitted to be active in money lending (forbidden to the Christians by the Third Lateran Council). This occupation attracted additional envy, wrath, and bodily attacks of the masses and increased the gap between Jews and Gentiles. Those who accuse the Jews of a self-imposed isolation should understand the history of the Lateran Council.

In addition to the theory of the "Witness-People," the constant effort of the Church to baptize non-Christians was a dramatic factor resulting in preserving the biological existence of the Jews. They had to survive in order to fulfill the hopes that the Church had put in their conversion. Even forced baptism was a world apart from the Final Solution. While the first could exhibit similar examples, the latter had no precedent in history.

The difference in executing anti-Jewish legislation was merely formal. As a super-state institution, after it became the state religion, the Church had suggestive lawmaking power only, which in turn had to be implemented by the state. In modern Nazi Germany, however, the legislative and executive power was in the hands of the same body. The advice of the Church sometimes got out of hand, but still there were curbs upon it. The Nazi system provided that the state assumes responsibility for the entire process: the passage of laws and their execution.

The Jews were considered "different" not only by the laws imposed on them, which isolated them in special quarters, distinguishing them by unusual garb and directing their activities into certain occupations and social degradation, but also because of certain real differences in their social and political attitudes. Their love for individual freedom, liberal and brotherly approach to all men, opposition to racial discrimination and to the personality cult, and their traditional condemnation of violence and crime, all generated a natural ideological opposition to the Nazis' ideology and political practice.

The Jews had no formally structured hierarchy similar to the Church or Nazi party. When attacked, they could respond not as a strong, unified international power (which they were accused of being), but only as an organized local community. They had no political influence at times when such pressures could have been life saving. Hoping to create the Messianic Age of man's brotherhood through justice and love, they could not subscribe to the totalitarian idea that any means is good to achieve a good end. Their goal and their means were right here on earth, built daily for everyone. This was, however, much different from their opponents, whose goal was also terrestrial. This distinction is even reflected in the national anthems of the two peoples: "Germany above everything" versus "Our hope is not yet lost to live as free people." The difference was also in comparison with the paradise "not of this world" being the final coronation of Christian religious aspirations.

The combination of this belief in not harming other human beings and of their own political weakness in a hostile environment influenced the reaction of the Jews to attacks. Instead of forcefully resisting, they tried to evade the enemy. Those who were on the top have often considered this cowardice. This, plus lack of real political power, made the Jews an easy target. The only strength the Jews had was in their God and in their belief that he was walking with them. And when this spiritual support weakened with the secularization brought by liberalism, the Jew had even less power to resist the pressure of the enemy. This Jewish position only further enticed the attacks of the Church and of the Nazi state.

On the other hand, a government seeking popular support offered the masses *panem et circenses*, an idea not new in buying public opinion: delivering the Jew was the fun-*circenses*, and his property was the bread-*panem*. Expropriation of the property of the Jews who had lived in some European countries almost as long as the host population, could add to the German resources, but was not a strong enough reason to annihilate them. In the past, Jews were robbed but allowed to go free, according to the example of not killing the cow that is being milked.

Compulsory transfer of ownership to non-Jews, Aryanization, had already removed the bulk of their business from Jewish control. The areas of industry, real estate, and transportation became aryanized first. The Jewish middle class was economically significant but not indispensable. Therefore, jealousy and hate of the wealthy Jews, ascribed to Gentiles, was only a minority situation. The mass of persecuted Jews was poor. This generalization seems to be reflected in Hannah Arendt's[1] evaluation of the people who attracted hatred because of their wealth (without support of power). She hopefully does not include in her "inter-European Jewish element" with its "useless wealth" the hungry, obscure Jew from Galicia. She sees as the source of modern anti-Judaism the historical process of the decline of the nation-state, which coincides with the loss of public function and influence by the Jews. They became a target of hostility in common with those whom they had served in the old form of government. As another reason, she presents the hostile relationship between the modern mob leaders and the Jews in whom they saw the central cause for all evils[2]. Arendt fails to recognize that such a mystic attitude of the mob towards the Jews can be explained only in terms of an already existing emotional situation created by anti-Jewish Christian upbringing.

Was this paranoia artificially created or were the Nazi leaders perhaps themselves paranoid and afraid of the real enemy? There is evidence that they were not afraid of the Jews. Discussing the Jewish question on November 12, 1938, Goering[3] remarked that he would not like to be a Jew in Germany. Kehrl[4] testified that Jews in Germany were in no way dangerous. There is also no evidence that Hitler's hate grew out of a real fear of the Jews. Thus, the official propaganda built up the already existing prejudices and enmity in Germany and in other countries to proportions having no relation to actual conditions. Nazi leaders knew that such emotions were widespread. Goering said that the Fuehrer would like to tell the Poles that they were acting against their own Jews in Poland[5] and to ask other foreign countries why they were always talking about the Jews instead of taking them in.[6] But how well he knew there was nobody to take the trapped people in!

However, with time, as the propaganda daily hammered anti-Jewish lies into the heads of the Germans, even the authors of those fabrications could not resist its power. Self-hypnotized, they started to believe that the Jews were their enemies. This belief grew even stronger after they began to expect vengeance from those whom they tormented and annihilated.

In his address at the Poznan meeting of SS major generals on October 4, 1943[7], Himmler, speaking of the extermination of the entire Jewish *race*, left no chance for any exceptions: "And they come, 80 million worthy Germans, and each one has his decent Jew. Of course, the others are vermin, but this one is an A-1 Jew. One could remain a decent man while killing women and children: To have stuck it out and at the same time-apart from exceptions caused by human weakness—to have remained decent fellows, that is what has made us hard. This is a page of glory in our history which has never been written and is never to be written, for we know how difficult we should have made it for ourselves, if with the bombing raids, the burdens, and the deprivations of war we still had Jews today in every town as secret saboteurs, agitators, and trouble-mongers. We would now probably have reached the 1916-1917 stage when the Jews were still in the German national body. We have taken from them what wealth they had".

That this was not a mad emotional act, but a deliberately prepared act of a new morality, Himmler stressed in these words: "Sober as we always were, truthful toward ourselves ...We had the moral right, we had the duty to our people, to destroy this people which wanted to destroy us."

According to Himmler, Jews were not the only impediment in the Nazi march towards world domination: "Then, when the mass of humanity of one to one and one-half billions line up against us, the Germanic people numbering, I hope, 250 to 300 millions and the other European peoples making a total of 600 to 700 millions (and with an output area stretching as far as the Urals or a hundred miles beyond the Urals) must stand the test in their vital struggle against Asia. But till then, in spite of the silly talk about humanitarianism, we imprisoned all this criminal substratum of the German people in concentration camps. What happens to a Russian or to a Czech does not interest me in the slightest. What the nations can offer in the way of good blood of our type we will take, if necessary by kidnapping their children and raising them here with us. Whether nations live in prosperity or starve, interests me only so far as we need them as slaves for our culture.

The other side doesn't make life easy for us. And you must not forget that the fortunate position in which we are placed by occupying large parts of Europe carries with it also the disadvantage that in this way we have among ourselves, and thus against us, millions of people and dozens of foreign nationalities. Automatically, we have against us all those who are convinced Communists; we have against us every Free Mason, every Democrat, every convinced Christian. These are the ideological enemies whom we have against us all over Europe and whom the enemy has totally for himself".

We do not need any additional evidence that the Nazis did not consider the Jews as their only enemies. Why then were only the Jews singled out for complete annihilation?

Nazi violence was a threat not only to the religious and ethical values of mankind as a whole but also to the biological extermination of particular groups—if not by way of the crematorium, then by way of atomic weapons, which they came very close to developing. While this is only a conjecture, the mass destruction of Jews had become a *fait accompli* of the past.

One would think that even the most brutal man would shed his animosity toward the Jews because of this catastrophe, and that their untold sufferings before their total annihilation would melt a stone. But this was not the case. The venomous sprouts of hatred were permitted to grow in Germany as well as in other countries and to become a spiritual obsession. The desecration of cemeteries and the painting of swastikas on synagogues by the Neo-Nazis are symptomatic of a continuous and perhaps incurable German mind. An even greater madness is evidenced by those who have grown up within the borders of our free society, the American Nazi Party: "Right now," they say, "the biggest of the Jew big lies is the incredible story that the Germans actually murdered six million Jews in cold blood." Like during the Nazi times, the presence of some intellectuals in their ranks legitimizes the neo-Nazi movement.

Chapter III

PSYCHOLOGY OF THE FANATICAL ANTI-JUDAISM

The Nazi era proves that intellect and science are not more powerful than instinct and prejudice. Only a strong moral and ethical backbone combined with an open mind can keep the "silent majority" on the road of righteousness, especially under the pressures of power employed by a totalitarian system. The highly civilized and intelligent German society lacked the moral determination to evaluate the Nazi ideology critically and objectively. Those who represented science should have been, by the very nature of their education and profession, opposed to any distortions of truth and usurpation of power in the name of a dogmatic political ideology. Instead, they sold themselves to the system. One of the greatest disappointments in human history arises from the group of the scientific community, namely, physicians, who broke the Hippocratic Oath, and in place of healing, assisted in torture and killing. While the repertoire of physicians-killers was limited, the rest of the medical profession knew what has been practiced and did not object to the criminal acts of their colleagues. Not only the politicians, or yesterday's great military heroes, or even the captains of the German economy but also those who represented science jumped on the bandwagon of the Hitlerian megalomania. Where, then, does this leave the man in the street, particularly when no condemnation came from the rest of the world?

But what could further exposes accomplish? Plenty was written and spoken about this subject. The only answer was a deep silence. The Western Christian civilization simply did not care one iota what happened to the Jews, even after the bloodbath of 1942. The outcry of the now shocked American Jewry did contribute to the State Department's initiative in calling the Bermuda Refugee Conference in the early part of 1943. However, the resolution proposed there considered it unfair to give priority to the Jewish question. Please read Nora Levin's *The Holocaust* and Arthur Morse's *While Six Million Died*, and you will see how well everybody knew what was happening and yet could not or did not want to help. We should repeat the statement of Henry Morgenthau, Jr. in which he accused the U. S. State Department of suppressing information and of calculated obstructionism.

There is no sense in asking those who were drowning in the whirlpool of persecution to publicize their situation when the western press was flooded with the news. The Allies not only refused to open their gates to Jewish emigrant masses, not only were they timid of naming the Jews as the primary victims of the Nazis, but also refused to bomb the crematoria and the railways leading to the extermination camps.

Analyzing the behavior pattern of the Germans during the Nazi era, one must come to the conclusion that there is not only one, single psychological factor solely responsible for their criminal acts. The theory of group sadism and "follow the leader" philosophy is certainly not the final solution to the question of the German personality.

Examining the psychology of the Nazi movement, Erich Fromm[1] stresses the relation of the German religious heritage to the German National Socialist movement. Fromm believes it was a foundation for the entire ideological system itself. The Germans' desire to rectify the injustice of the Versailles Treaty is easy to understand, but their insatiable lust for power, conquest, and destruction under Hitler, out of proportion to any injury they had suffered, is perhaps the product of their national character and individual traits. Even without the historical cause-the Versailles Treaty-Fromm thinks, the Germans were inherently capable of committing crimes.

Fromm sees the role of the Protestant Church as a dominant factor in molding the anti-Jewish character[2]. Protestantism, like the Catholic Church, believes that man cannot find salvation on his own merit but needs the grace of God. By breaking with the Church and rebelling against the Pope's letters of indulgence, Luther made the Protestants independent and more self-sustaining in religious matters. However, in freeing himself from Church dependency, the Protestant became even more submissive to God. The absolute surrender to Divine power later led to the idea of submission to the secular leader. As that leader's authority grows stronger, the masses relinquish many of their freedoms. This, in turn, contributes to the formation of the authoritarian character of Protestantism. In examining the principles of Nazi theory, Fromm finds that the concept of inherent inequality originates with Calvin's theory of predestination: no matter what one does in life, some people are born to be saved, others are destined for doom. Thus the Protestant who became independent from the Church and from medieval society because of the doctrine of predestination desired to replace his submissiveness with sadistic tendencies and destructiveness. His suffering manifested itself in masochistic or sadistic behavior, usually unifying both characteristics. The masochistic trait found its revelation in the submission to the Fuehrer and satisfaction in the Fascist ideology. The latter is achieved when the leader is successful. Thus power and success are a precondition of this system. The sado-masochistic character tries naturally to eliminate the object of its hatred.

Fromm sees in the lower middle class of Germany and of other European countries the sado-masochistic character, which on the one hand needs an authority to lead it, to submit to, and on the other hand craves for authority over others[3]. This kind of personality is representative of Fascism in its social and political form. Hitler appealed to the masses because he personified the vengefulness of the lower middle class. At the same time he promised German industrialists and Junkers and other members of the upper class things which could never be fulfilled. The Junkers and big capital responded to these promises and thus played a vital part in establishing Nazism. The success of the new party had to be demonstrated at home before it could win on a foreign battlefield. An easy solution for attaining it was the pillaging of Jewish property, liquidation of Jewish businesses, and the elimination of Jews from important positions. The masochistic and sadistic ideas transplanted from the religion into politics found satisfaction in Hitler's dream: German masses would be kept under the strong arm of Hitler and the Nazi bureaucracy, and they (the Nazis) would exert power over other nations and dominate the world. In his plan to destroy the fictional enemy, Hitler accused the Jews, communists, and plutocrats of proposing the same plans that he was soon to enact.

For Hitler, the destruction of the Jews had to be a total one. It had to be a holocaust. There was no pity; there was an absolute contempt for lack of power. As for his people, he would give them the satisfaction given to masochists. There had to be a complete submission to himself, the Fuehrer. The individual meant nothing, that is, he meant only as much as he served the ideals which were represented by the leader, who himself submitted to God, Faith, Necessity, History, and Nature. Thus,

Fromm finds in the Fascist character a complete destruction of individualism and a submission to a higher power.

Fromm's analysis of German psychology does not allow us to better understand the sadism of the Ukrainians and the Lithuanians who cooperated with the Nazis, or the sadism of Polish pogroms, of Chmielnicki's massacres, and of the centuries of persecutions by people other than Protestants. It creates confusion in appreciating the great sacrifice made by a very few Germans, such as Provost Bernhard Lichtenberg, and very many Danes, almost all of whom were Lutherans. It cannot claim the exclusiveness of Protestantism in molding the sado-masochistic attitude toward life since we saw the atheistic KGB in Russia and the political police in China also exhibiting these character traits.

The deep-seated emotional implantation of hatred by the Church, a conditioned reflex of behavior, appearing in special situations of socio-economic crises and violence, was further augmented by Martin Luther's teachings. It was easy to use this long cultivated sentiment of hatred for the same ethnic group, even when the Nazis turned against the Church. German Christians, before Hitler, could expect salvation on a par with others; now, in addition to this, they were placed on the top of the racial pyramid at the same time, as the pinnacle of the superior Aryan race. Since scientifically they could not prove that the Jews, whom they labeled the most inferior race, were anatomically or intellectually less valuable, they exploited the old sentiment toward the Jew-God- killer in order to bolster their pure blood theory. As such, a carrier of eternal condemnation, the Jew could not escape from his situation even if he tried to do well. He was simply responsible for all evil.

The Jew became a symbol. As the second world war developed, Germans saw that world conquest would be difficult to achieve, in spite of their greatest efforts. When the tide of the war eventually turned against them and the racist mirage of world domination became unreachable, they felt they could at least have the satisfaction of the destruction of the symbol of their foe. The new order turned against the western powers and against their civilization. The Jews were the oldest witnesses and midwives of that civilization. A nation, which based its relation to others exclusively on the actions of force of its storm-troopers, had to turn against those who had brought with them from Sinai inhibitions against human violence.

One could not have it both ways: when man rejects God's law in a society based on inequality and forcible expansion, concentration camps and mass executions are unavoidable. When the executioner becomes the lawmaker, and there is no freedom of appeal and of free speech, what else could be expected? When the political monster kills individual freedom, the uncontrollable frenzy of conquest replaces all. When every greeting is *"Sieg Heil!"* there can be no concern for justice and no consideration for innocence.

Many young people and some older ones compared American involvement in Vietnam with the tactics of Nazi Germany. By no stretch of the imagination are the violent acts committed by the U.S. government in the Vietnamese war comparable with those perpetrated by Hitler's Germany. And yet, what an outpouring of protests! How many demonstrations were there at that time in Germany? How many burned their draft cards? How many set themselves on fire? How many members of the legislature attempted to alter the policy of the government?

This kind of protest never happened in Germany, not because Germans were cowards. They were not. Many died for Hitler. The fanatical anti-Judaism of Hitler and his clique could be successfully transplanted only in the minds of a people in whose psyche the anti-Jewish sentiments were already deeply rooted. This was not only the result of Hitler's hypnotic power and the successful propaganda of Goebbels. There were more long-standing and deeply rooted sources.

Nazi propaganda chose blood from all other tissues because of the mystic attributes ascribed to it by the masses. Blood "binds" people and makes them blood "relatives;" it divides them or becomes a symbol of the enemy whose blood is sought in vengeance. It symbolizes one's temperament and sexual drive when it is said that "he has hot blood." Blood is hidden in the vessels of the body. It is unseen. False anatomical differences ascribed to a "mother race" can be easily verified. They are visible.

Hitler's theory of pure superior German blood and an inferior, corrupted Jewish race was nothing new; however, under his leadership it became a religious belief of National Socialism. The masses accepted it without reservation. In their frustrations, they seized the opportunity to take it out on others. The *Herrenvolk* was slowly recovering from the World War I defeat, discarding their inferiority complex, a by-product of the Treaty of Versailles. Mass arrests, desecration of the Jewish holy places, plunder of their property and the slaughter of innocent people—all these took place while the Germans stood by unaffected, giving wholehearted support to Hitler. These chauvinistic aspirations were fed by a host of pseudo-scientific theories that came from people purporting to be authorities in the field.

In a paper, Otmar Freiherr von Verschuer[4] tried to summarize the Nazi's "scientific" findings on the race biology of the Jews. The work is a mass of contradictions and confusion, as is the rest of Nazi research. To begin with, von Verschuer contends that the idea of a pure race cannot be applied to Jews according to scientific anthropology. Jews are derived from the roots of different races. As a multi-racial conglomerate they exist in opposition to the pure German race. The amazing phenomenon, that this nation without a state could survive two thousand years was a result of both their racial ability and their blood separation. A common religion, specific upbringing through the Talmud and the idea of being chosen to educate by example prevailed to such a degree that in spite of conversions to Judaism by many individuals and groups, the specific character of the Jews did not change.

Comparing the inherited and adapted characteristics of Jews with those of the Germans, Verschuer admits that the differences are not often apparent. He goes on to ascribe certain body features, diseases, and psychological traits found in some Jews, to the entire population. He stresses the nose, "die Judennase," the same way *Der Sturmer*[5] did, bent on the end and similar to the number "six" in profile. The body movements and specific race odor, similar to garlic, which the Jews like, distinguish them from others. While at first he says that their characteristics made them easily recognizable, he states further on that, of course, one cannot expect that each Jew fits this type; only a small minority qualify for such a definition. He refers to a study by Virchow in which the incidence of blond hair, blue eyes, and light skin among German children was 31.8%, among Jewish 11.2%, while the dark skin, dark hair, and brown eyes occurred among German children 14.3% and among Jewish 42%.

Finally, he admits that not too many Germans fit the pure "nordic" racial characteristics either bodily or psychologically.

It does not matter if spiritual Jews can be recognized by their bodily characteristics. After describing the incidence of certain diseases and psychological deviations among Jews, Verschuer curiously admits that Jews were less involved in criminal acts than the rest of the population, particularly in the case of theft and bodily assaults.

He ends with the description of the character and spiritual values of the Jews. For example, they isolated themselves from the host people, and thereby, in spite of statelessness and dispersion, they preserved their national identity. They have a racial peculiarity not seen in any other group of people, and therefore one is justified in speaking about a Jewish race. (What an unsuccessful tautology-attempting to prove the proposition by labeling the Jews with an unfounded adjective-not born out by previous biological considerations—and then using it as a proof of the Nazi race theory!) And a repeated denial that Jews are a race follows. Jews were not agricultural but tended to be urban instead. They preferred to be active in commerce not because of external forces but as a result of their own inclination.

Talmudic education taught them logic and shaped their choice of professions. The religious and "national" idea of being a "chosen people" helped the Jews isolate themselves and preserve their racial distinctiveness. The Jew does not base his life on instincts or on the unknown, but believes only in this world, in what he is able to comprehend with his intellect. In such a world there is no place for true faith and love.

In the same volume, another professor, F. Burgdorfer[6], presents tables proving the high incidence of crime among the Jews in Germany, primarily in the area of petty frauds and misdemeanors. This data show that in general Jews were committing crimes out of their proportion to the entire population. Particularly significant is the high percentage of racial disgrace, *Rassenschande,* in the years 1936-1940. Those were the times of the enacting of the Nuremberg code and of Nazi terror. Nobody can imagine that many Jews would, under those circumstances, dare risk their lives to "stain German blood and German honor."

How much credibility do Nazi statistics deserve? Though to us they seem ridiculous, in a frenzied desperate society they were proof that the hereditary criminality of the Jews was actual. The press and radio daily bombarded the receptive German masses with stories of murders perpetrated by Jews for thousands of years. The idea of the man-killer readily replaced the old form of God-killer. There was no possibility of a critical assessment of the true situation. The party line was domination of fantasy and instincts in contrast to the Jewish "rationalization". Pseudo-scientific icing covered the extraordinary propaganda cake for which the Germans showed a voracious appetite. A compilation of Schramm's *Der Judische Ritualmord*[7], for example, fed their warped desires. The Nazis needed anything regardless of its credibility that could "confirm" their ideology and, in particular, fabrications about the ritual murders committed by Jews.

Though the Nazis turned against organized religion when it suited them, they utilized the Church-created demonology of the Jews. According to the Nazis, the persecution and even murder of those who were born evil, killed the Christian God, desecrated the wafer symbolizing Him, killed Christian children to re-enact Christ's suffering, and poisoned wells was allowable and guiltless. This was an appeal to the atavistic anti-Judaism. One could not rationalize. On the contrary, there were scientific attempts made to prove that Jews were different. The anatomist Hirt of the University of Strasbourg examined Jewish skulls to show that their sub-humanity was apparent in their bone morphology.

While the ritual murder[7] accusations dated back to 1144 AD and were responsible for locally organized Jewish massacres, newer fabrications of a Jewish world conspiracy created a much greater danger to Jewry. By constant secret manipulations, it was alleged, Jews had attained economic and political power in order to be able, finally, to rule the world. As nonsensical as they appear and though proven to be forgeries, these fantasies of the *Protocols of the Elders of Zion* appealed to the receptive masses then, and are still now in circulation.

In Germany, especially, the soil was ready for the new seed; Luther and the race theoreticians of the nineteenth century had prepared it. Heinrich von Treitschke's saying "the Jews are our misfortune" became a daily expression. He said: "...they appeared as terrible blood-suckers of the German peasantry" [8]. Racial supremacy of the Germans, preached for decades not only by Germans but also by foreigners, only needed Hitler's agitation to explode into the exploitation of the "inferior races." The Frenchman, Gobineau, and especially the Englishman, Chamberlain, wrote about the mastery of the Germans in creating the real values. Therefore they deserved the distinction of a "master race" and the non-productive parasite races could rightfully be exterminated.

Martin Luther taught that the parasitic races included "the murderers of Christendom."..."that they be forbidden usury and deprived...all jewelry in silver and gold. And this is the reason: All that they possess, they have stolen and robbed from us by means of their usury.... Let them earn their bread in the sweat of their noses.... It makes no sense, that they wanted us, damned Goijm, to work in the sweat of our faces, and they, holy people, should spend lazy days behind the oven, celebrating and eating." [9]

The crassness of this lecture in economic jealousy had great appeal, particularly during times of depression. Religious and economic attacks were combined effectively with the race theory and utilized by the founder of the Christian Social Workers Party, Adolf Stocker; the founder of the League of Anti-Semites, William Marr; and the philosopher Eugen Duhring. In essence, Luther and these men were the fathers of Nazism, teaching not only the abolition of Jewish rights, but also the uprooting of Judaism and the extermination of this "depraved race which destroys the culture." They became the ultimate historical source for many German writers and scientists.

Germans had heard such theories for generations. Therefore, it is hardly possible that the Germans could be stunned by Hitler's racial theory. Hitler does not deserve the credit given to him by many for creating the race theory. There is evidence[10] that he did not believe in race in the scientific sense, and that he needed this concept only as an intellectual basis for his "new order."

On the other hand, the instinct of self-preservation in the Jews had been lulled by the existence of the repeated call for their destruction: they were sure that, as before, the call was only a metaphor for the abolition of their rights.

The Germans too might have doubted Hitler's call for the annihilation of the Jews and therefore they did not resist. It might have been true for some of them. But they were the active participants in this cosmic game; they had the choice of decision, and they chose to stand religiously behind Hitler.

Luther's teachings concerning Jewish attempts to rule the world were strengthened by the appearance of outside "evidence" in the form of the *Protocols of the Elders of Zion*.

Norman Cohn[11] discusses two anti-Judaic approaches. One, related to the role played by Jews in a certain society, is less dangerous, never leading by itself to genocide. The other, based on fantasies about Jewish conspiracy and collective embodiment of evil, is the exterminatory type. The mythical *Protocols* reflect modern, complexed, virulent anti-Judaism. In the eyes of a fanatic the silhouette of a Jew with the mysterious and supernatural attitudes ascribed to him during the Middle Ages is compounded by everything frightening in modern life. Cohn speaks of fanatical anti-Judaism as a matter of unconscious negative projections. This means that people read into the behavior of others the anarchic tendencies, which they fear to recognize in themselves.

Fanatical anti-Judaism disregards Jews as individuals and projects on Jews collectively the images associated with an unresolved Oedipus complex. The Jew is seen both as a "bad" son and a "bad" father, potential killer of the son, castrator, and torturer. As their name indicates, the Elders of Zion are supposed to be father-figures who do to nations what the son imagines the "bad" father is doing to him. The Jew, in a sense, castrates the son-nation, using its resources for its own benefit.

If the myth of Jewish world-conspiracy could be understood in terms of the Oedipus complex, one would expect it to be an unconscious fantasy, which it was not. It was well described, and it was very real. Cohn's statement that many men who never stop being small boys with respect to their emotions, and continue to see the multiplied "bad" father as monsters incarnated in other people, cannot be applied to the Germans calling, "*Heraus mit den Juden*," Out with the Jews, and later, "*Todt zu den Juden*," Death to the Jews.

If the historical relationship of the Jewish people to Christianity and to Europe makes it almost inevitable, as Cohn says, that Jews should be seen as a kind of collective father-figure, one would look for a similar relationship in other genocides. It cannot be found, for example, between Turks and Armenians preceding the slaughter of over a million Armenians during the years 1915-1916.

Cohn discusses a theory of Ernst Simmel, in which the latter concludes that the Nazi anti-Judaism was an expression of mass delusion, in fact, of a mass psychosis of a people afraid of Jews. The unrestricted aggressive destructiveness under the spell of a delusion, in complete denial of reality, is the paranoiac form of schizophrenia. However, the Nazis consciously denied reality; they lied. Therefore one cannot explain their behavior by aberration of mind. The Holocaust was the ultimate expression of decay of moral standards. Only if one assumes that violation of accepted morals and ethics (God's law) is a criterion for mental deviation can German crimes be an expression of psychopathology. Nazis were, contrary to Simmel's theorizing, normal people who committed abnormal crimes to such a degree that they were afraid of becoming abnormal as a result of this experience. Hilberg[12] discusses this when he refers to von dem Bach's warning to Himmler that Kommando members were in danger of becoming either neurotics or savages.

Hilberg feels that the executioners in the Kommandos and the bureaucrats participating in the destruction of European Jewry had the same morality as the rest of the German people. The executioners themselves were not specially trained or chosen, and no use was made of professional killers. Any lawyer in the RSHA (*Reichssicherheitshauptamt*) or any finance expert could be chosen for the deadly task. Furthermore, there was no serious opposition from the population at large. Moral scruples were overcome by a conscious use of obscure rationalizations and psychological repression.

In order to conceal the reality of its program the Nazi bureaucracy proceeded through five stages of repression. The first was secrecy to keep knowledge of the destruction among participants only; the second—to make sure that all those who possessed that knowledge participated in the process, becoming accomplices in the crime; the third—to prohibit criticism of what was going on; the fourth—the suppression of social conversation on this subject; and the fifth—omitting mention of "killing" or "killing installations" even in secret correspondence.

The justification of extermination was achieved first through propaganda, calling for the boycott of Jewish goods or to come to mass meetings; second, by declarative propaganda to combat guilt feelings for the perpetration of criminal acts. This was achieved by repeating the old saying that "the Jew is bad," repeating the theory of Jewish world domination and of plots against Germany, by statements that foreign statesmen unfriendly towards Germany were Jews or else related to them, by saying that the Jew who created capitalism and communism was responsible for the war effort of the Allies and the terror raids, and that the process of annihilation was a form of preventive war.

In addition to the above general rationalization, Hilberg divides rationalizations into five categories: first—the doctrine of superior orders (the *"Befehl ist Befehl"*) was like absolution; second—the action was not performed because of personal vindictiveness; third—that one's own activity was not criminal, that the next person's action was criminal; fourth, one's action was insignificant because it was only a small part in the great machine of destruction; and fifth—all life processes in nature depend on conflict in which some individuals or species must necessarily perish. Pseudo-scientists who distorted the historical facts and scientific data attempted the support of some of the justifications mentioned by Hilberg.

German science and German institutions of higher learning never opposed the Nazis, and often served them with great enthusiasm. The masses found in them the authority of distortion instead of the objectivity of truth. The law of the jungle which grew up on dark instincts would never have led to a catastrophe of such great proportions if it had not been supported by doctors, professors, technicians, and other respected professionals. The professional intelligentsia and the German academic community were as much to blame as the killers themselves.

The efforts of these experts followed the party line. They tried to prove that a Jewish conspiracy was attempting to gain control of the economy and culture in order to undermine Germany. Another road, supposedly chosen by the Jews to achieve this goal, was through direct criminal acts against the Germans. A published work entitled *Forschungen zur Judenfrage*[13] co-authored by a number of German professors, attempted to prove this thesis.

When liberal ideas swept through Europe, Jews naturally embraced them. Heine, Borne, and Marx, three prominent Jewish apostates, were presented as proof that Jews not only remained under the spirit of the French Revolution of 1789, but also that they opposed the early chauvinists of the nineteenth century. Heine, Rothschild, and Marx were supposed to embody the three forms of Jewish hegemony of that century: the literary, the financial, and the socio-economic.

Professor Botzenhart[14] of Gottingen calls Heine a "dangerous type", disloyal but not hating Germany so openly as Borne. If these two Jews loved Germany as much as they maintained, why did they insult and ridicule all German values? The answer, according to Botzenhart, is simple: they were striving for a Germany founded on the liberal movement—a spiritual branch of France and at the same time a spiritual branch of Judaism. They wished to reverse the assimilation of Jews into Germans. This was, says Botzenhart, the real reason why the two writers felt so strongly about the ideas of 1789- a reason of which they were not conscious themselves. The international Jew led by Heine, Borne, and Marx fought over the fate of Germany, using his financial and spiritual powers. His control of the press often determined the acceptance or rejection of a book. His real power was so different from the often abrogated legal privileges that, for example, the Jew in Vienna, though hardly tolerated, was a deciding political factor.

Botzenhart goes on to claim that while the Jewish magnates ruled the finances, the small Jews ravaged the population in a manner hard to imagine. Those who introduced liberal amendments favoring Jews were under Jewish pressure, like Metternich, or were corrupted, like Buchholz. The Jews planted those who fought for equal rights. The prince of Hesse, for example, who sanctioned the first equalization of the Jews in Germany, did business with Rothschild. The Jews built not only their financial but also their social and political strength, using the influence of their salons. A new one, not less demonic, replaced the old order of wars and emperors, ruled by gold. The emergence of the Rothschilds was proof that the old stories about Jewish power were based on fact.

Botzenhart quotes Treitschke's historical objectiveness: "This cradle of liberation of Jews soon became the home of the fanatic hatred of the Jews, who became vampires of the German people."[15]

Pleyer discusses the role of Jewry in capitalistic society.[16] He found the liberal concepts of economic development lacking in that it excluded the factors of race and nationality. Sombart[17] was the first to describe the relationship of the factor of race to economics. He saw in Jews the perpetual money-lenders and the founders of modern capitalism.

Pleyer cannot digest Sombart's expression: "Israel moves through Europe like the sun: wherever he comes a new life is born; from where he leaves, all that blossomed fades."[18] In the development of European capitalism two types appear: the producer, developer, and organizer being one; the businessman, salesman, the second. Germans represent the first type, and Jews the second. Though they have had other opportunities, Jews by their racial nature are inclined to be salesmen and bankers. Accumulation of capital gives them money power. In their commercial activities Jews go even so far as to stimulate the demand for certain goods artificially. The exploitation inherent in capitalism is a "bad example" for the Germans, creating habits similar to those of the "white Jew."

The influence of Jews grows in proportion to the growth of commerce and to the decline of production. Jews use talmudic methods in business, and in spite of the fact that there were some Jewish judges to side with them, Jews were often punished for breaking the law, says Pleyer. While undermining the economic and legal structure of society, the Jew simultaneously uses the Marxist appeal to the workers. Jewish property in Germany was estimated to be about twenty billion Reichsmarks in the form of stocks and bank accounts. It was a Jewish trick, says Professor Pleyer, to base Jewish economic power on a piece of printed paper; but it was also a weakness in that the fate of the Jews hung from that piece of paper.

In addition to capitalism Jews used Bolshevism to undermine and finally blow up Germany. So went the Nazi theory which applied the sign of American dollars and the Hammer and Sickle to the Star of David in the caricatures of *Der Sturmer*, and found support in the paper of Richthofen[19]. According to him, Bolshevism depends upon the support of the Jewish spirit. The founder of the communist idea, Karl Marx Mardochai, left his legacy to the practitioner Lenin, who probably was of Jewish descent. Stalin, who inherited the power from Lenin, carried Jewish blood in his veins. His maternal grandfather was a Jewish dealer in second-hand goods.

There was a great participation of Jews in important Russian institutions according to Professor Richthofen who simply named many of them and labeled them Jewish. The scientists, writers, and artists who opposed the Lenin--Stalinist line were liquidated with the active participation of Jews. The Bolshevik method of deception and propaganda was based on Jewish principles according to Richthofen. Bolshevism followed in particular the Jewish view that it is easy to release man's lowest instincts in order to exploit him. Jews who supposedly did not subscribe completely to Bolshevism were using it for their own goals to achieve personal power. An example was Leon Blum. Writings of Jewish authors also had a decomposing effect on the structure of societies—for example, Ilja Ehrenburg's influence on the Spaniards before their civil war. This Russian writer in his book, *Dayosh Evropou*, gave a special expression of Jewish hatred for Gentiles and European states, envisaging with sadism the victory of the final battle of the world revolution. The patriotism shown by the Soviets in their fight against Germany was nothing more than a red tactic inspired by the Jews, who were also responsible for Stalin's allying himself with the Anglo-Saxon plutocrats. The ruling clique surrounding Stalin consisted of Jews, and the persecution or liquidation of any one of them was only a political maneuver—all this according to Professor Richthofen.

A much greater and immediate danger to the Germans, however, was the cancerous spread of the foreign Jews within the national body. Although the number of people professing Judaism was half a million in Germany, two hundred thousand in Austria, and twenty-seven thousand in the Sudeten, the total number was actually one to one and one-quarter million, according to Burgdorfer[20], if one adds the non-religious half- and quarter-Jews. About one-fifth of them were foreigners or stateless. Their natural growth showed a decline in total numbers—a condition that would have suited the German ideology perfectly.

However, the rational Jewish approach to sexual life and birth control also affected the Germans. Jews were responsible for preaching about the free will to propagate and for the fight against so-called compulsory motherhood, using the spoken and written word, the theater, film and press to undermine the sexual morality on which marital and family life depend. The Jews were the ones who either practiced or supported the crime of abortion. In doing so they were pretending to consider the misery of the masses, but actually they were leading a war against the national interest. Those who distinguished themselves thus were the physicians Magnus Hirschfeld, Levy-Lenz, Sigmund Freud, and others. These individuals, says Burgdorfer, succeeded in paralyzing the will of the German people, accusing all those who indicated the danger of the declining birthrate of being militaristic or nationalistic.

While weakening the Germans biologically, the Jews also attempted to gain economic power and influence. They were encroaching upon commerce, the free professions, especially the healing arts, science and entertainment. There were only about nine per cent Jewish laborers within a forty-six per cent total labor force; less than two per cent of the Jews worked on farms as compared with twenty-nine per cent of all farm workers. In commerce only a little over eighteen per cent of the total population was active as compared with sixty-one per cent of the Jews. Sixteen per cent of all lawyers and eleven per cent of all physicians were Jewish.

This concoction of a little truth and a lot of distortion was served to the German masses by those who supposedly carried the torch of truth. Their teaching is very close to Martin Luther's. Compare the above mentioned condemnation of physicians bent on destroying German lives with Luther's paranoiac cry that Jews, especially Jewish physicians, would kill all the Germans if they could.

Thus, the power of the word has a potential to ignite fires, which can devour nations and all mankind. Any decent human being would feel a revulsion to torture and to kill innocent people- and so would the German. Sympathy can, however, be replaced if there is a strong effort to present the victim as a monster, "like bacteria and vermin."[11] The public can become hyposensitized to crime through propaganda and example. Hyposensitization is achieved by mixing truth with its distortion. First, partial lies are spread. After they have been accepted and the ability of critical evaluation is thus disturbed, obvious lies are offered, sometimes by the authority of those who represent religion, science, or political power. Small lies are gradually built up by propaganda, thereafter supported by terror and intimidation to such a point that the brain-washed citizen accepts with ease a dose of news which would have shocked him at first. Even the most aware populace can accept the most violent ideas in this way.

The second form of psychological hyposensitization of the German people was achieved by gradual exposure to violence. Over thirteen million members of the Social Democratic and Communist parties were overpowered: those who were not beaten learned to live according to the Prussian saying, "*Maul halten und weiter dienen*" (to keep their mouths shut and go about their own business).

After establishing the dictatorship of one party, the "new order" extended its brutal control over the economy. While retaining private enterprise, the Nazis imposed directives and restrictions upon it, abolished trade unions, and did away with the Jewish businesses. Little resistance was offered against these initial maneuvers. Then came the first great purification of the party ranks, which took the life of Ernst Roehm, the leader of the SA, and, thousands of his adherents. In addition to the vigorous support of Hitler, who promised a thousand years of a mighty Reich, a fear took over the German hearts. If the vanguard of National Socialism could be exterminated so easily, how much easier was it to accept a similar treatment of other segments of the society, especially Jews, who were the "internal enemy"?

The next hyposensitizing booster of German conscience was "eugenic medicine." Over one hundred thousand Germans categorized as "defective" and "useless" to society were killed by German physicians. Though this was a supposedly secret undertaking, many knew about it, but only a few dared to raise their voices in protest. Werner Heyde and over fifty other physicians conducted this euthanasia program during the years 1939-1941. But, Hitler's plot to murder the epileptics, the very old, and chronically ill members of the master race was already known in 1935. Those who ask Jews, forewarned by Hitler in *Mein Kampf*, why they remained in Germany until it was too late can direct the same question to the victims of "eugenic medicine" who did not dare take the threat seriously.

There was a law for "protection against inheritable disease" which was written before the anti-Jewish Nuremberg code. The administrative headquarters of the euthanasia program received cooperation from hospitals, which prepared lists of chronically-ill patients who were often delivered with a full knowledge of their impending death.

About half a million people were sterilized after 1933. Karl Brandt, Hitler's personal physician, supervised the euthanasia of the undesirable people in German society, paving the road to "The Final Solution." Killing German children with carbon monoxide, lethal injections, or overdoses of morphine or barbiturates hyposensitized many of the doctors cooperating in the project, to the eventual mass murder of Jews. Those who seek an answer to the question: How could an average German permit this to happen? should also ask themselves how persons who were supposed to devote their lives to comforting and healing could partake in killing. Physicians used their positions of power to carry out horrible experiments, well aware that they break the Hippocratic oath. Submersion of people in freezing water, implantation of bacteria and glass into human muscles and similar atrocities condemned those "healers" in the annals of history for all times.

The appalling killing of masses of Jews and the sadistic experiments on living human beings by hundreds of German physicians and paramedical personnel make it imperative to review and re-evaluate the requirements of a physician with special emphases on his moral principles. If the color, creed, nationality, or political persuasion of the patient conditions the improvement of health and the prolonging of life, let the doctors say so and discard the Hippocratic Oath. If a physician may be a henchman and kill a part of the population in order to give more "*Lebensraum*" to the rest, let it be admitted openly. Otherwise, a sharp demarcation line will have to be placed between the noblest profession and those who learned the science but changed the art of healing into killing. The mere repetition of the news from the lay press, the digestion of historical data, or what is more common—running away from the subject—are not going to answer the basic question of the medical student as to the moral attitude he has to take as a physician. Until now there has been no official condemnation of the criminal physicians by the profession. Indeed, many of them who escaped the gallows, or did not commit suicide, were still practicing medicine in this hemisphere and elsewhere in the world after the war. There were, of course, many more doctors who were criminals in Nazi Germany than the few hundred on official lists, but even against the latter the medical world did not take an official stand. Why?

There was not one protest then. Not one of the famous physicians committed suicide to set an example, though many Nazi doctors did so after they lost the war. The apologists of those times might say that the medical profession had not incurred the wrath of the public, which was unaware of "selections" and medical experiments. But the profession knew it well.

During medical meetings in which hundreds participated, atrocities were discussed. It is known that the doctors realized that these experiments were not performed according to medical ethics. At one such conference from May 24 to May 26, 1943, Professor Gebhardt stated that he assumed full human and political responsibility for the transplants of bones which was performed by Fritz Fischer on Polish women in Ravensbruck. In addition, the profession learned about experiments from, for example, a book published in 1943, by the neurologist Georg Schatten, based on his transfer of encephalitis from monkeys to a number of mental patients.

It was shown that all the criminal experiments made in the name of German medicine and research did not promote scientific progress one iota. For this period in Nazi medical research Leo Alexander proposed the term 'science of killing.' And there was not one critical voice inside Germany to try to stop this licensed murder.

The World Medical Association, after it condemned the crimes of German physicians at its first assembly in Paris, urged the German medical profession to take this opportunity to clear its name. It asked for a formal statement from the Germans admitting that certain physicians "violated the ethical traditions of medicine, defiled the professional medical honor and prostituted medical science by placing it at the service of war and political hatred."[21]

A trial of German physicians opened on December 8, 1946, and the judgment was ordered on August 19, 1947. During that time the incredible events were established "by clear and public proof, so that no one can ever doubt that they were fact, not fable, and that this court, as the agenda of the United States, and as the voice of humanity, stamp these acts, and the ideas which engendered them, as barbarous and criminal...."[22] The guilt of the German physicians was and is undeniable.

In order to prevent recurrences of "eugenic medicine" and medical experimentation, every medical school must put aside some time to tell the story of the infamous Nazi doctors and to teach and repeat to every graduating class the moral and ethical obligations of a physician. The official stand of the profession has to be clear and known. On the twentieth anniversary of the end of World War II the editorial staff of the Journal of the American Medical Association_ reviewed a paper asking that such a stand be taken. The answer was as follows: "American medicine took a clear stand more than 20 years ago by its contributions to medical service during the war. Twenty years later you would have us wave a flag and say, 'It's official'. " Perhaps this is necessary, so that no one should forget the crimes of the past; otherwise, medical doctors participating in *Sonderaction* are a possibility in the future.

Dr. Elie Cohen[23] feels that people like Kremer, Mengele and Hoess were normal individuals with a criminal superego. Additionally, he finds an explanation for this in Freud's group psychology. The superego is the weakest part of the personality in some people, he says, because of a lack of intellect and a disturbance in the maturing of their personality. Cohen thinks that the superego of many Germans was different from that of other people, as, for example, Netherlanders or Jews. Therefore, the latter were unwilling to believe the wartime stories about gassing, and non-Jews after the war could not believe in concentration camp atrocities. Cohen believes that the German superego, which developed into a criminal superego when Hitler's ideas took possession of it, was responsible for indifference rather than outright, active hatred and hostility against the Jews.

The criminal superego compounded by the authoritarian character structure led to a new type of man represented in German life by Adolf Eichmann. As Gideon Hausner[24] describes him, he carried a mask till the end. The external niceties were without doubt all-important for him. Though responsible for the lives of millions, he repeated that the duties performed by him were not the cause of actual murder. In the courtroom, while watching pictures of the indescribable horror for which he was responsible, he was so insensitive as to respond only to his appearance in front of newsmen without his proper attire.

Quoting from Sassen's manuscript, Hausner describes Eichmann as saying that he had never had a bad experience with a Jew, that the enemy was not persecuted individually, and that it was a political matter. He carried out his program with all the fanaticism that an old Nazi would have expected of himself, and that his superiors undoubtedly expected of him. They found him to be the right man in the right place.

Another representative of this Nazi type was the arch-technician of death, Rudolf Hoess, commander of Auschwitz. He is described by Gilbert[25] as an apathetic little man whom nobody would have suspected to be the greatest murderer ever. He responded to all questions in a mechanical matter-of-fact way. He showed no emotional reaction, relating how he had executed Jewish families by trainloads on Himmler's orders. Though Gilbert suspected some schizoid features in Hoess, he felt that they were not necessarily responsible for his behavior. Rather it was the force of the Nazi police state: the militaristic authoritarianism and racial ideology produced a new species of schizoid murderous robot.

To put the previous discussion in a capsule form, one may conclude that the Nazis' German potential to perpetrate the near-annihilation of a total people was a criminal superego formed by centuries of anti-Jewish teachings by the Church, by Martin Luther, by race theoreticians and others—all reinforced, magnified and emotionalized by Nazi propaganda.

As mentioned before, economic motives could not be the pre-eminent cause of the Holocaust. However, they were thoroughly involved in the "gravy" the Germans collected from the Jews on their way to the chimneys. After robbing the Jews of their possessions, the Germans used them as free labor to supply their war machine and simultaneously to torture and break Jewish morale. Oswald Pohl, for example, who headed the branch of the Ministry of the Interior, suggested in a letter to Himmler dated April 30, 1942, that an unlimited workday would be a convenient form of "non-violent" extermination. Millions, before they died, were exploited by such institutions and industrial concerns as DEST (Deutsche Erd- und Steinindustrie), DWB (Deutsche Wirtschaftsbetriebe), I. G. Farben, Krupp Werke, Herman Goering Werke and others; they built fortifications, anti-aircraft trenches, tunnels, railroads, etc. Malnutrition, injuries, and diseases thus competed with Zyclon B, shooting, and intracardiac lethal injections as a means of extermination.

Cohen[26] proposes in part that the cruelties inflicted by the SS camp personnel, because of the lack of restraint strengthened by the pent-up aggressions of an authoritarian education, was possible because of the absence of "psychical counter-forces." The authority of the external world, which normally provides these counter-forces, now in the form of National Socialism, encouraged the extermination of the inmates of the camps. Cohen believes SS violence to be an expression of pent-up frustrations. This analysis recalls Fromm's discussion, presented in the beginning of this chapter.

Germans wanted to remember the injustice done to them at the close of World War I, but they did not like to discuss the part they played in precipitating the events. Their drive toward the East (*Drang nach Osten*), their refusal to permit the Austria-Serbian dispute to be settled peacefully, and their declaration of war on Russia, were all things they did not like to discuss. They also remembered the Treaty of Versailles. Even if they were innocent of precipitating World War I, directly or indirectly, and suffered injustices at the hands of the Allies, why did they have to take out their wrath on the Jews and not, for example, on the French?

Hitler's *Mein Kampf* was the final call to set fire to European Jewry. But long before this the Germans were prepared for such an act by Gobineau's *Essai sur l'inegalite' des races humaines*, Chamberlain's *Grundlagen des Neunzehnten Jahrhunderts*, and by many other writers closer to the grass roots. In the German people, in addition to anti-Judaism, there had to be implanted an anti-humanism of some form, allowing them to relate to others with little regard for the value of human life itself. This could be only achieved through an insidious, subtle alteration of the instinctive appreciation of life , or to use Nietzsche's expression-the transvaluation of values.

The theories of the philosophers made the German mind ready for those new values. Fichte taught them about a society built by individuals without moral limitations. Germans are chosen to build such a society. Hegel saw sense only in the constant conflict of the vicious circle: thesis-anti-thesis-synthesis. As a form of conflict, war not only makes sense in itself, but it is also desirable as a race-moral purifier. Nietzsche shared these views. He compounded the glorification of violence with images of heroism and of the messianic mission of masters gaining satisfaction through bestial murder.

Chapter IV

THE VICTIMS

Were the Jews in any sense responsible for what happened to them? Did they bring it on themselves? In the first place I find the posing of these questions sacrilegious, even if they bring into focus the slightest suspicion of the culpability of the Jews in their own destruction. This possibility has been raised and as yet it has not been universally denied.

There are additional related questions: Were the Jews ever completely guilty or completely innocent? Did they contribute in any way to the lack of respect accorded them by the society in which they lived before the Hitler era or during that era? Did they participate in their own annihilation by committing suicide or by killing other Jews of their own free will? Were there any possibilities of escape or resistance, which they failed to employ? Why do I consider posing the questions sacrilegious?

Simply because even the most guilty among the Jews had not, at the time of their execution, committed a crime punishable under any legal code by torture and death. The Nazis condemned them only for being Jewish and not for committing any active crime. While most of the previous religious persecutions would let the Jew preserve his life for the price of conversion to Christianity, the racial oppression gave him no chance to change his mind. He had no alternative to a death prepared by criminals in utmost secrecy and recognized only when the showers of Zyclon-B were turned on.

Some consider the change of mind of the Jew from assimilation to complete apostasy as a factor responsible for an increase in German hatred. The period of emancipation and assimilation coincided with the growth of German racist theories. The attempt of the Jews to assimilate themselves within the host nation was described as a devilish trick whose purpose was to undermine the German society, and likewise, intermarriage was an attempt to poison German blood. While Jewish "friends" supporting the Jews as individuals, but demanding their dissolution as an ethnic entity, called for complete assimilation, Jews of their own volition cooperated and accepted their host's religion in great numbers, leaving not only their own, but often joining hands with their Christian "friends" to break up the files of those who remained true to Jewish morals and peoplehood. An example was Karl Marx, who generalized, calling religion the opiate of the people, but who was also very specific when speaking about Jews in his *On the Jewish question.*

Those apostates were not fully accepted by the Christians and drew upon themselves the abomination of the Jews themselves, because they considered Christian baptism as a ticket to the executive's office- a step up on the social ladder. Some openly admitted this, and, like Heine, could not completely sever their ties with Judaism. The number of apostates from Judaism in the nineteenth century, according to Ruppin[1], was at least a quarter of a million in the world, twenty-two and a half thousand in Germany. Thus Judaism lost many brilliant minds. Frequently they betrayed their religious brethren without reason.

The French Revolution and liberalism further increased the area of contact between the Jews and the rest of German society, opening new opportunities of growth and education for them, and removing the dam holding back the waters of creativity. The conservative elements opposing the equality of all citizens was eventually forced to capitulate to the progressive majority. However many continued to disbelieve in the inherent equality of all men-a belief central to the liberal's social code.

Having always been predominately urban, the Jews had no greater historical or economic reasons for moving out of the cities after the emancipation than other city dwellers. Naturally they engaged in professions common in the cities. In criticizing them for this, one cannot compare the percentage of Jews engaged in farming with the absolute number of German farmers, but one should ask, rather: What is the number of Jews compared with the general urban population that turned to the soil? Besides, the opportunities granted to them by liberalism were not restricted by any occupational conditions. Quite to the contrary, forcible direction into specific vocations was directly opposed to the liberal ethic based on free social and economic competition. And it is true that Jews showed themselves efficient in this competition and reached a great importance in Germany's culture and economy. Their contributions were so monumental that even their enemies could not deny the obvious facts.

But when it came to an evaluation, the contributions of individuals were those of the citizens of the country and not of the members of the Jewish community. The Jewish share in common German efforts did not help to establish a better Jewish-German relationship; on the contrary, it resulted in further alienation. Perhaps successful competition in a free society and outstanding contributions to the common welfare were reasons why the Jews had to be annihilated?

In addition, the Jewish community was blamed for the active role played by individual Jews in politics-people who openly denied any ties with this community and frequently maliciously attacked it. These individuals on the left or on the right were "punished" by brutal murder. But this was not enough for right-wing extremists. The writer Kurt Eisner of the Social Democrats, the communist leader Rosa Luxemburg, the representative of the government, Walther Rathenau - all were killed by the Germans who never could forget that they were of Jewish descent, though they often acted against the interests of the Jewish community. There was an immediate "reflex" action of the well organized mob who went about plundering Jewish shops and homes and beating Jews. This premeditated exercise in so-called justice was only a prelude to an elaborate propaganda expose of Jewish treason and the "stab in the back" theory.

Were those individual Jews who were active in politics real traitors to the German people? Yes, claimed the Nazis, although they could not prove it. Ziegler[2] presents Walther Rathenan as a person who was definitely condemned by the Nazis, but whom we see as a German patriot and a great statesman. Since he was a typical German Jew, and even more German than most Germans themselves, his case is of further interest. In his article, "Hear, Israel," at the turn of the century, he appealed to Jews to change their background, attitude, and behavior and become not only German patriots but even a little bit chauvinistic. He described them as an Asiatic horde, which lives too close within itself, and is separated from the rest of society by a self-imposed ghetto. The Jews were not part of the nation, but rather a "foreign body." He wrote: "Look upon yourself in the mirror. You used to say, you cunning, that who owns riches, owns power. Now you have the riches, but the rich among you are less regarded than your poor. Your rhetoric was vain... You organized yourself for defense instead of for integration... They will charge you of being international as long as you are related to the foreign Cohns and Levis. Forget the exotic cousins and relations.[3]

These words should have pleased those Germans who demanded a complete assimilation. But Rathenau went only that far. He neither called for conversion nor himself became a convert to Christianity, and he never failed to identify himself as a Jew. He wrote: "I fight against the injustice in Germany.... The injustice exercised against German Jewry and partially against German citizenry is not very great, but it exists. Therefore it has to be spelled out." Many of his letters express the following sentiment: "I feel German and will never separate from my German people." How much more assurance could one expect from a man who was a genuine German patriot?

The story of Rathenau's political activity is well known. During World War I, he became the founder of the department of raw war materials, and later, secretary of state. In spite of all apparent correctness, according to Ziegler, his heart did not support the German cause. However, there was no basis to suspect this man of a lack of sincerity. But despite his great achievements for the state, the Germans killed him as an enemy of the people.

After they had lost the war, the Germans spread the "stab in the back" theory. Shirer[4] writes that this was a fraudulent legend. General Ludendorff, the High Command leader, insisted on September 28, 1918, on an armistice "at once," and his formal superior, Field Marshal von Hindenburg, supported him. The German Army had maneuvered the republican government into signing the armistice and accepting the Versailles Treaty. Even Ziegler[5] says that Rathenau opposed the signing of the treaty. In spite of this, the belief that Jews and Marxists were responsible for the "stab in the back" persisted and was soon to aid in Hitler's rise to power.

In the program of the Nazi party another lie, based on Hitler's speech in April, 1923, claimed that Jews caused World War I. The delirious masses believed this and supported the Nazis under a flag with the inscription: "Deutschland erwache" (Germany awake!) with the cry, "Juda verrecke" (Perish, Judah!). They who supported the *Drang nach Osten* and *Lebensraum* wars launched by their government found it necessary to accuse somebody else of starting them. Were the Jews responsible for the war or for the misery that befell Germany as a result of the Versailles Treaty? Obviously, the historical facts deny it.

We have reviewed the attempt of German Jews to blend with the society in which they lived. Assuming that this was not successful and not universal, and that Jews, by separating themselves and by their external appearance, irritated and stirred up resentment in the Gentiles, was this, perhaps, a sufficient cause for abusive treatment, torture, and death? Is this the price one has to pay for not conforming, for being or appearing different, for having long hair, a different garment, black skin?

The Christian apologists would like to alleviate the burden of their sin by sharing it with the Nazis only so far as it showed theological coloring, and also by having the Jews themselves share in the final responsibility. Any such attempt cannot be substantiated by facts and puts the apologists and the few hysterical Jewish writers who try to place the innocent victims in the same camp with the Nazis. Jewish complicity in anti-Jewish acts in the fourth and later centuries is based exclusively on the writings of those who themselves perpetrated those acts and burned Jewish books; Jewish co-responsibility for the Holocaust is a creation of Nazi propaganda and is believed only by those who still remain under its spell.

Eichmann and Sassen tried to invent a justification for the Final Solution. They presented a diabolically clever Jewish scheme, in which the Jews became instrumental in their own slaughter, according to Hausner[6]. International Jewry, primarily Zionism, provoked Germany to destroy the Jews, in order to claim statehood later on. In order to secure their national existence, they were willing to sacrifice their own blood. Only insanity could be receptive to such a theory or to the suggestion of Eichmann's lawyer, Dr. Servatius, that irrational motives beyond human understanding might be the basis of the bad luck of the Jewish people. Even an insane person who could believe with Eichmann that the Jews committed suicide would then have difficulty understanding his joy of achievement when he said: " I shall jump into my grave laughing, because the fact that I have the death of five million Jews on my conscience gives me extraordinary satisfaction"[7].

In view of this exclamation, how could Hannah Arendt[8] or Jon and David Kimche (whom she quotes) ascribe to the Jews complicity in their own extermination? Even to come closer to this monstrous lack of logic one has to study the Nazi anti-Jewish activities in two stages divided by the period between September 21, 1939 and July 31, 1941. Before that time the Germans did not know themselves how to solve the Jewish question in Europe. Though murder had been committed, as, for example, in my city of Przemysl, where about eight hundred Jews were killed in 1939, a massive deportation to Madagascar or Israel was still considered. Arendt says that during the first years after Hitler's rise to power the Zionists believed that the emigration of Jews to Palestine would be a "mutually fair solution," an attitude described by Arendt as "non-criminal cooperation." Following her train of thought, any society that tries to rescue people being expelled from another country is cooperating with that country. For example, West Germany's taking in Sudeten Germans after World War II, Israel's receiving Jews expelled from the Arab countries could be cited as cooperating with those countries doing the expelling.

Nonsense! Any attempt to rescue Jewish lives or property on the part of the Palestinian Jews at that time can only be praised as simple human decency. Not only the Zionists but even the Germans did not know, during that stage, that the Final Solution would take place, and Miss Arendt admits this herself. Therefore, no wonder that young people were picked first to be transported to Palestine, where hard work and pioneering in the desert were more suitable for the young than the old. How can the selection of people for work in communal settlements in Palestine be associated with a situation years in the future, when deportations were organized from the ghetto to the death camp, or, as Arendt puts it, when the non-selected majority of Jews inevitably found themselves confronted by two enemies—the Nazi authorities and the Jewish authorities? By the same token, her attempt to minimize Eichmann's crime by reference to the Kimches obviously refers to the time when Eichmann's participation in the Nazi "purification" of Europe from Jews had not yet entered the stage of the Final Solution.

This Final Solution "was mentioned" by Heydrich at a meeting on September 21, 1939, outlining the concentration and starvation of Jews in Polish ghettos. The final plan for the total annihilation was prepared on January 20,1942 at Am Grossen Wannsee in a suburb of Berlin.

This decisive break should make anyone, including Arendt, conscious that "the banality of evil ," as she calls it, lost any features of banality at that point and became a sub-animalistic, devilish venture. At that moment the Jews of Europe had lost the slightest chance of independent action. Broken by terror, beatings, and starvation, they found themselves in the situation of a crowd in a burning theater—everybody trying to save himself even if, by chance, he should step upon the fallen body of another. But, admirably, how very few stepped upon the bodies of the fallen! Only those who were there during the hellish years of 1942-1945 have the right to sit in judgment. The armchair philosophers should remain silent. They know no comparable standards, nor have they experienced a more abysmal situation, which would qualify them to criticize Jewish behavior in those days.

If by collaboration one understands the willing and conscious assistance given to the enemy, then there was none from the side of the Jews. Those who "collaborated" were few in numbers and did it only under extreme duress. I remember the days before the organization of the Jewish Council, the so-called *Judenrat*, with the wild chasing and beating of Jews on the streets, and the seizing of Jews for work groups, when the Ukrainian police under the German eye were using riflebutts and whips on young as well as old. The chaos and terror were so great that one prayed for some kind of relief organization. The institution of the *Judenrat* was important not only as an administrative body but as an organization responsible for law and order in those lawless times. It protected the Jews from policemen and soldiers of other nationalities who were collaborating with the Nazis. The primary necessities of life, food and lodging, were obtained only through those authorities after all rights were taken away from the Jews. Certainly, there were abuses of their positions by some Council members, or by the Jewish militia. Jews are people, not angels, and any deviations from accepted ethics can be expected among them as among other humans. But for any cases of such deviation there were many examples of unusual nobility among the Jews.

In elaborating on the role of the nation-state in Jewish history, Arendt states that without the interests and practices of the government, which was maintaining Jews as a special group, Jews could hardly have kept their group identity, though there did exist coincidentally a Jewish interest in self-preservation and group survival. This, of course, is not true: the Jewish group identity also existed under political systems other than that of nation-states, often under conditions amenable for assimilation and opposing the external drive to it. I like Arendt's criticism of the scapegoat theory. I consider this a tautology of the idea of innocent suffering. She believes that the so-called scapegoat, the innocent victim which was singled out, ceases to be innocent when this label is applied. Men, wishing to escape punishment for their own sins, blame an uninvolved group or individual.

By the use of these expressions the anti-Jews escape responsibility, and the Jews do not wish to discuss their share of responsibility, says Arendt. She believes that modern anti-Judaism has been connected with the assimilation and dissolution of the old religious and spiritual values of Judaism, and that Jews accepted anti-Judaism as an excellent alternative to keep their people together. Though, as a result of anti-Judaism, Jews indeed kept closer to each other, from Arendt's description it appears that they invited and welcomed anti-Judaism, and that thus they were also culpable. This is nonsense. She sees, in the exploitation of the existing anti-Judaism, a means of the Nazi regime to win the approval of the masses for its totalitarian methods of choking any resistance. In order to keep the wild enthusiasm of a chauvinistic world conquest growing and to divert attention from the real difficulties, the artificially created paranoia of the lurking Jew was cultivated.

Hausner[9] describes some of the persons who at any time and under any conditions could be pointed out as luminous examples of human virtue. For objections to German demands, *Judenrat* chairmen were shot. Many committed suicide rather then "cooperate" with the Nazis-for example, individuals like Adam Czerniakow in Warsaw, Dr. Joseph Parnas in Lwow, and entire groups like the *Judenrat* in Bereza Kartuska. The resistance of these heroic men did not stop the deportations or postpone the liquidation of camps or ghettos. The power of the enemy was so overwhelming, his authority and terror so great, that nothing done by the Jews could lessen the number of victims, as Arendt imagines. Many *Judenrat* members risked their lives by bribing Nazis in attempts to mitigate the terror of the

Germans. There is also plenty of evidence that some *Judenrat* members were active in the underground.

In connection with the preparation of Gestapo lists of different categories of ghetto dwellers, the *Judenrat* was fooled until the very end, as was the rest of the population. The first lists were of those who belonged to the labor brigades—young people who, because of their contributions to the war machine, received additional food rations plus the promise to be allowed to stay longer on their jobs. During the great deportations of 1942 people wanted to remain in the ghettos. Nobody knew the real destination.

To be on the list of workers and to possess an *Arbeitsschein* (document to work) was a temporary blessing. All others had to go. The Germans did not need the *Judenrat* lists. All Jews were registered, concentrated in a small area, and always available. The number of those for deportation was simply the difference between the number of working men subtracted from the total number registered.

Nobody ever knew what the Germans planned in any given situation; once the people on the list might be destined for work, another time—for death. When we recognized that the Germans had deceived us and were taking us to Auschwitz- -and not to work—it was too late, and no lists were necessary. Members of the *Judenrat* shared the fate of others in "resettlement" actions.

Arendt hints that Jewish Sonderkommandos (special units) had committed criminal acts but answers herself by adding "in order to save themselves from the danger of immediate death." These acts on the part of the Sonderkommandos constituted an automatic, animalistic, life-preserving behavior pattern. One cannot apply the accepted ethical or psychological yardstick to those who were physically abused and spiritually destroyed. It is impossible to comprehend this unless one has had this experience.

We can help to make such a situation understood by comparing it with similar happenings. For example, the well organized and highly trained Russian soldiers, especially the political officers, let themselves be slaughtered without any resistance. They, too, had their Kommandos in camps. I saw tens of them throwing themselves on a scrap of food, fighting to get it. From their camp in the village of Pikulice, next to Przemysl, I saw them once being led by a few German guards with empty carts. When they returned, many carts were filled with corpses. Germans described some of the Russians as cannibals, and displayed their pictures, purporting to show that they would eat the buttocks of freshly-dead comrades.

There are further examples: the great hunger in Russia when mothers were devouring their children's flesh in 1922, or the following quotation from II Kings 6:28: "This woman said unto me: Give thy son that we may eat him today, and we will eat my son tomorrow. So we boiled my son, and did eat him: and I said unto her on the next day: Give thy son, that we may eat him; and she hid her son."

There is no reason why an historian should accuse the Jews of guilt for acts which they would never have committed under normal circumstances. What is more, we must condemn these historians for putting the oppressor and the oppressed on the same level, and for being unable to differentiate between cooperation and forcible submission. *Judenrat*s were forced to become Nazi servants-it was more than a necessary evil..

Of course there were a few individuals among the Jews-as there are in any society-whose behavior bordered on gangsterism, but no Jew at that time can be accused of crimes with intent to destroy the Jewish people-which was the purpose of Nazi persecution.

Though Jews always had a great solidarity in the internal affairs of their communities through loose but respected organizations, they were unprepared to have a unified mechanism of action on a pan-European scale during the Nazi era. The myth of Jewish conspiracy and strong international organization has been destroyed by one of those who knew existing organizations very well and who had a chance to study them before doing the destroying. The head of the Anti-Partisan Units, the Higher SS, and Police Leader on the Russian front, Erich von dem Bach-Zelewsky[10], testified after the war that the Jews had no national or international organization whatsoever. It was one of the greatest lies of anti-Semitism-that Jews conspired to dominate the world through their strong organizations. If they had had any sort of organization, Bach said, they could have been saved by the millions. Instead they were taken completely by surprise.

This evaluation of Bach's is highly exaggerated. There was some organization of the Jews in existence other than the *Judenrats*. But even if the Jews had been more organized than any civilian society, even if they all had had a military organization and had not lived in unfriendly surroundings, they could not have helped themselves. They were in the same position as the masses of Russian prisoners of war that let themselves be killed without the slightest resistance, right up to the time that the Germans incorporated them into Vlassov's Quisling army.

Incidentally, of great interest is what Bach had to say about another anti-Semitic lie of the Nazis, namely, the friendliness of the Jews for the Soviets. He calls this allegation the most appalling misconception of all. The Jews of old Poland were never sympathetic to communism. Those who lived east of the river Bug were more afraid of Bolshevism than of the Nazis. Of course they were, they remembered the Russian pogroms.

No wonder so many contradictory answers were received to the present question on Jewish responsibility. Historians themselves, not satisfied by the presentation of factual crimes of such dimensions, tried to pin the suspicion of co-responsibility on the Jews for some insidious reason. In particular this pleased those of the non-Jewish world who tried to lessen their own responsibility.

The name of Hannah Arendt became a slogan for apologists such as these. But even Father Flannery,[11], who has tried hard to find Jewish coresponsibility, says that Miss Arendt seems to press this principle too far at times. I have previously quoted Raul Hilberg, whose book, *The Destruction of the European Jews*, is considered one of the best on this subject. Unfortunately, the author introduced some very daring and false concepts into which he attempted to fit historical facts. Much of his information contradicts his own interpretations. He also misrepresents the facts themselves and thus distorts the historic truth. If anybody was caught in a straitjacket, it was not the Jews whom he accuses of plunging themselves physically and psychologically into "catastrophe," but the historian himself who expresses such an illogical idea.

Nathan Eck[12] proves step by step that this is so and points out how facts and myths may lead to premeditated slander rather than historical objectivity. Though Hannah Arendt and Raul Hilberg may consider themselves good Jews, their work not only damaged the Jews, as did Nazi propaganda, but does not conform to the findings of scientific and historical research. Enough time has elapsed since critiques of their work appeared in print. If they felt that they made mistakes in the past, they should have come forward and not been silent.

Eck writes that Hilberg's description of the Jews lining up for the deportation trains, seems to make it appear that the victims did it of their own free will, for the sake of convenience—not because they were forced and had no alternative. Hilberg's charges that the Jews had forgotten the act of revolt appear to apply to the entire people, to the nineteen centuries of Diaspora including the Nazi era. Instead, he says, they learned submission and acceptance of their fate. This became such a habit that, as a part of their nature, it made it impossible to rebel against the Nazis, who could not have succeeded in carrying out their plans if the Jews had forcibly resisted. The only exceptions were the Jews in ancient Palestine and Israel. Eck asks: who are these Jews in Israel? Were they not immigrants from the Diaspora, many of them survivors of the Holocaust? Must we not conclude that the people remained what they were and that only the conditions changed? Hilberg develops his idea further, accusing the Jews of acceptance of the anti-Jewish regime and attempting to survive with it, maintaining that they migrated only when expelled by force or economic depression. They tried to live through pogroms and they made an attempt to live with Hitler. They stayed because of the passivity of their 2,000-year Diaspora.

I, myself, remember the severe winter of 1939-1940. I lived on the border next to a Russian frontier police outpost. Several hundred yards from me was the frozen river San dividing the Germans from the Soviets. For days in the beginning I saw groups of refugees, mainly Jews, herded off by the Russians. Later, the border was sealed off, and those who dared cross the ice were shot upon reaching the opposite shore. I present my own case as a confirmation of Eck's statement that there were many Jews who jumped from transport trains and lived as "Aryans" or hid in the fields or in the forests. Not only did I jump off the train but so did my 67-year-old mother, who was shot.

Eck denies Hilberg's assertions. The Jews did not know that they were destined for death. Even if Hilberg were right in saying that by late summer of 1942 almost every inhabitant of Poland had some inkling of what was going on, it was already too late. The overwhelming majority of Jews in the occupied territories had been murdered during the great "actions" in July and August of that year. Even though they lacked any knowledge of their real fate, the Jews had already started preparations for an armed revolt before the end of 1942. The masses of Jewish people did not know what awaited them till the showers of Zyclon B were turned on. The Germans used deceit, forcing deportees, before their extermination, to write postcards to their families and friends remaining in the ghetto about the good working conditions, the special camps for children, and the abundance of food. The henchmen responsible for the slaughter of thirty thousand Jews in Babi Yar, says Eck, bore witness during the Nuremberg trials that the victims believed down to the final moment before their liquidation that they were going to be transported to some other place, thanks to an illusory " wonderfully clever" organization.

The Germans promised the starving Jews food in their new setting. Their officers gave their "word of honor" that the new place offered better living conditions. As a result, some volunteered to be deported from Warsaw. But the majority had to be forced to the trains. Nobody from my city offered himself for deportation. Indeed, many were shot, along them the head of the *Judenrat*, Dr. Duldig, for refusing to cooperate with the deportation planners.

Eck blasts Hilberg's contention that the role of the Jews in their own destruction was more important than the cooperation of the army and the attitude of the civilian population. He points to Hilberg's distortion of the facts based on his susceptibility to Nazi propaganda. Actually, the Nazis were responsible for all the ills of the ghetto, including the depraved character of the inhabitants. In spite of the few small successes, Nazis found Jewish morals and ethics stronger than their brainwashing and terror. The vast majority of Jews could not be broken. Eck decries Hilberg's misrepresentation of Jewish courage and resistance. Hilberg uses generalities such as the one concerning the insignificant number of German casualties caused by Jewish armed opposition. He specifies only sixteen dead and eighty-five wounded in the Warsaw ghetto uprising, and no more than eight dead and twelve wounded in Galicia. Thus, Hilberg erases the results of Jewish armed resistance in the forests, in the camps, and in the ghettos. The fact that one of the Jewish partisans who lived after the war in San Francisco related to me, that in only one of his military encounters, twenty-four Germans fell, and that another, Z. Kremen of Ramat Gan, Israel, blew up twenty-two German trains, is ample evidence that Eck's criticism is valid. Eck points out that Hilberg is not only using misguided concepts and a fictional theory about the Jewish mentality in general (how close to Nazi stereotypes!) which he labels "Diaspora passivity," but also gives false information in order to support his distorted attitude.

Finally, Eck tries to understand Hilberg's motivation. He suspects that a deep, emotional involvement of the author, his particular disappointment and frustration, resentment and anger, pain or hate of himself or of the whole people, or even love could pervert not only justice but also the historian's judgment.

As mentioned before, we Jews do not have illusions of faultlessness or perfection. We do not, however, have to apologize for the relatively few cases in which there were Jewish transgressions against fellow Jews in the ghettos, nor for the very few historians who distort the truth. Certainly the onus of guilt for these crimes lies on those who were directly responsible for them and on the rest of the world which exhibited such apathy—and not on the Jews. If any Jew—and particularly an historian—has a feeling of guilt, it must be neurotic. Guilt lies with the persecutors, not with the victim

Chapter V

HELPLESSNESS

In spite of the bitter experience of centuries of persecution by the state, the Jewish tradition of law and order still evidenced a great effect on the Jewish masses. Rabbi Hanania said in the *Wisdom of the Fathers,* III: " Pray for the welfare of the empire because were it not for the fear it inspires, every man would swallow his neighbor alive." The protection given to its citizens by the government compensates for their obligations and sacrifices in its service. Rabbi Hanania could not foresee a monstrous state in which the greatest cruelties against its citizens could be perpetrated. No tyranny in his day, or before, reached the insane evil of the modern totalitarian state. Why, then, faced with a new reality in the shape of the Nazi policy, did the Jews still follow Hanania consciously or habitually? Could they not have rebelled? Did they use their rights to speak out and act effectively?

In order to be able to answer these questions with any sense of perspective, one has to know what transpired before the catastrophe of the '40's. The Jews were gradually deprived of their rights over a period of five years. According to Blau[1], one hundred eighty-four laws were enacted between 1933 and 1938 removing the Jews from public life, from the national economy, from the slightest influence a normal citizen could exercise on his government. The rest of the citizenry had been intimidated and psychologically prepared for a violent treatment of the Jews, who became isolated, degraded, and exposed to the physical abuses of the mob and party henchmen. Jews are a sensitive people, and they were very well aware of what was going on. They did not live in a "fool's paradise" as Arendt describes it[2]; those who could do so, like herself, left the country. Those who remained behind were trapped; they could not leave. At first, when the Germans wanted to rid themselves of the Jews, the emigration doors were closed; thereafter, they became objects of bargaining between the Nazis and the West, which did not want to allow their entrance to begin with, much less pay for them as hostages. Until the Conference at "Am Grossen Wannsee" on January 20, 1942, no one had suspected genocide; neither the West- nor even Western Jewry would allow themselves to be cornered by German blackmail. If the West, so it was thought, would let the Jews into Madagascar or any other colony, there would be no Holocaust. Neither at that time, when they did not know, nor in 1943, when they all knew about the annihilation of the Jews, would the Western Powers give any assistance to the condemned masses.

In 1938, a crucial year in the fate of Europe and of the Jews, even Hitler had not yet decided on the "Final Solution." In his conversation with Pirow on November 24[3], referring to the *Kristalnacht* victims, he said that he wished to point out that he had no assassinations on his conscience. He had never adopted these methods. As a matter of fact, he presented himself as a protector of the Jews. The murders committed could not be ascribed to the National Socialists; perhaps other national groups were responsible. The world could not imagine what might happen in Germany if he, Hitler, were to withdraw his protecting hand from the Jews. If the West—including Western Jewry-did not know, if the Germans did not know, and if the Nazi elite including Hitler himself did not know, how could the Jews have known?

Without exception, all the Western Powers adamantly opposed a large-scale Jewish emigration to their home countries or their colonies. With such an attitude, all their sympathies and attempts to find a solution on an international level, (for example, during the Evian Conference of 1938) were merely a fusion of anti-German propaganda at the expense of the Jews.

Western Jews supposedly rejected Schacht's plan asking that the Jews outside Germany raise one and one-half million Reichsmarks for the release of German Jews. They were opposed to establishing a private committee, which would seem to prove the existence of something called "World Jewry." They believed that this was a matter to be considered exclusively by established governments[4]. There was probably another reason: a doubt that the Nazis would live up to an agreement with Jews, whose human rights they had violated.

While no direct transaction was concluded between the Nazis and the Western Jews, the latter did not merely sit on their hands. They did attempt to mobilize public opinion and to stir the interest of governments in the defense of their trapped brethren. The *Comite' des Delegations Juives* succeeded in presenting the case of German Jewry to the League of Nations. The American Jewish Committee and B'nai B'rith decided to deal through their own government and received pacifying words instead of effective action. The American Jewish Congress evidenced a more independent initiative. In general, the action of the Western Jews was timid and not well organized. They lacked a unified plan of procedure. However, why should the Jews of that period have been expected to take a more powerful and determined stand when the very governments of Europe which were- directly threatened by the Nazis retreated in appeasement before the German pressure?

From a practical standpoint, the Western Powers used their condemnation of the Nazis for propaganda purposes only. But at least they spoke out, and each country accepted a token number of immigrants. Pope Pius XII remained mute.

How should the Jews have combatted a threat which made the Western Powers shrink, which broke the Treaty of Versailles, occupied the demilitarized Rhineland, grabbed Austria, raped Czechoslovakia and invaded Poland, France, etc.? Could they have spoken up? To what avail? To speak up in that regime meant concentration camp confinement even for Germans, and for Jews such boldness meant certain death. To refuse an order in a totalitarian state is less of an offense than open criticism. To ask for one's rights is contrary to the philosophy of a state based on the violent suppression of freedom.

Since they had no way out of the country and were not allowed to complain, what else could the Jews have done? Did they have to live in the ghetto? Could they not have dispersed and become lost in the sea of Gentiles rather than remain concentrated in one area? Could they perhaps have assumed the identity of Aryans and thus escaped their fate? Could they have hidden themselves in Aryan homes?

No. The Jews had to live in ghettos. To be found outside the ghetto was punishable by death, unless one could prove that they were travelling to or from work. They could not hide. There were books in both the Jewish and community registries with the exact data about each individual. During the Soviet occupation of eastern Poland, Jews were considered a nationality and had this indicated in their passports, as did every other citizen in Soviet Russia. This passport was exchanged for the Jewish identification card, the *Kennkarte*, after the German invasion. One could not ask for a Polish or Ukrainian *Kennkarte* without turning his passport in. Let us assume that a person risked death and lived successfully without a *Kennkarte*, avoiding checkpoints. He had to have enough money to buy food on the black market as well as the other necessities of life, for all official rations could be obtained only with the identification card. One had to register merely to have a roof over his head. The greatest risk was from the local population. Full of hatred, they knew better than the Germans how to recognize a Jew. The hunted, hiding man would either be robbed, beaten, or murdered, or turned over by an informer to the Germans, who rewarded such acts with increases in the size of food rations. An informer, then, could easily combine the satisfaction of his greediness with a patriotic deed-ridding Poland of Jews. The occupied countries swarmed with informers, particularly Poland, a traditionally Jew-hating society.

Nevertheless, there were Jews who managed to survive in surroundings worse than a lion's den. They were those who were able to obtain an Aryan *Kennkarte* (I lived as a Roman Catholic Pole for over ten months).

Even in those times, there were Christians—Germans, Poles, and Ukrainians—who risked and sometimes lost their lives to save a Jewish one. These are the real Christian saints; they are also "Jewish saints." Thus, a small number of Jews were able to survive. However, this was impossible for most.

In a totalitarian society registration is a basic requirement. The checking of the number of the registered was a daily routine in labor battalions and concentration camps. Barefoot, hungry, tired, and beaten, hundreds would stand for hours on a frosty, snowy night until their number was verified. A notorious example is the registration of German Jews in the month of June, 1938. Four lists were prepared—each for a different branch of the administration: for the Gestapo, for the local police, for the criminal police, and for the internal revenue office. On July 22 of that year identity cards were issued, -even to Jewish infants; and on September 29 all Jewish passports were marked with a "J." Thus, there was no way to escape from the efficient surveillance of the German police.

There was another factor, which should not be forgotten. During the time preceding the "Final Solution," Jews experienced a totalitarian grinder such as no human beings had ever before experienced. They were completely deprived of all their possessions and broken spiritually. The final goal of the Nazis was to break them psychologically. To accomplish this they employed abuse, exploitation, and any violence short of death. And if we add to this the deceit of the Nazis, who fooled the Jews till the last moment, we can better understand why active resistance in the form of an armed rebellion could not take place en masse.

Sporadic anti-Nazi assaults, though they did occur, were limited by the fear of massive retaliations. The sense of responsibility for the rest of the community directed the attention of young men to the results of the assassination of Ernst vom Rath in the German Embassy in Paris. The Kristalnacht, "'Night of Broken Glass," followed. The balance of that night came to 36 Jews killed, 36 seriously wounded, 20,000 imprisoned in concentration camps, 76 synagogues totally destroyed, 191 heavily damaged by fire, and 815 shops reduced to ruins.

In my ghetto in Przemysl, the notorious Reisener attacked a young butcher, Krebs. Krebs disarmed the bloodthirsty Nazi and injured him with his butcher knife. The next day the Gestapo descended on the ghetto, firing wildly at passers-by. In addition, they took 25 hostages, whom they promised to release after the capture of Krebs. After they had caught and hanged Krebs and two other youths that attempted forceful resistance, they shot the hostages.

Why, then, did the Jewish masses not break out of the ghetto and flee into the forests to swell the numbers of the partisans? Moshe Kahanowitz[5] supplies an answer. In the first place, in order to quickly escape the pursuing Germans, such an attempt could only have been made after overpowering the police who stood guard, and in areas close to forests. Only the young and strong could have accomplished that. This would have provoked an immediate retaliation against those remaining behind. Close family ties and a tradition of mutual protection reduced the initiative of those able to flee to a minimum. Assuming that the total population of the ghetto succeeded in escaping (which would have been highly improbable because of the high walls, barbed wire, guards, and watch-dogs), how could children, elderly or sick people have survived the hardships of a life in the forest?

Some could have saved themselves and fled from the ghetto with the help, perhaps, of the local population. Unfortunately, the overwhelming majority of the Christian population was not interested in saving Jewish lives and often collaborated with the Germans. In fact, at times "friends" opened their "hearts" and hid the Jews only to rob them of their possessions, or even kill them. Instead of the good will and active assistance of the neighbors, there was very often open hostility.

To have any kind of viable defense, Jews needed arms. After repeated searches by the Germans and local police, it became impossible to hide weapons. Even so, some pistols were bought and smuggled into the ghetto by the more daring. The Red Army, retreating in 1941 before the German onslaught, left behind large quantities of arms, collected and concealed by farmers who could help the Jews not only with food and information but also with arms. Yet they refused. The weapons that were purchased for a fantastic price had to be concealed, usually outside the ghetto. Informers would either notify the Germans or try to blackmail the purchaser.

Those who, against all odds, succeeded in forming partisan groups tried to join or cooperate with the Russian partisans who were well trained, with professional leaders and the support and advice of Moscow.

The forests and marshes east of the Bug River made it easier to escape from the German penetration. However, the areas of central Poland and Galicia were flat lands and did not offer such a natural protection. After I fled from the train, I traveled through villages and forests for about a month in a futile attempt to find the Russian partisans. The right-wing Polish partisans, the "Armja Krajowa," which not only refused to accept Jews but also often liquidated them, constituted another dangerous obstacle in this part of the country.

Later on, when I lived under an assumed identity among the Poles, who themselves suffered immensely, I would hear them say, "Hitler deserves a monument for ridding Poland of Jews." The hatred in those people was stronger than their need for unification against a common enemy.

In territories belonging to Russia before the outbreak of World War II, the Germans did not give the Jews a chance to evaluate the situation, for immediately after entering the area they killed them. If under these conditions there remained Jewish partisan groups organized to fight the Germans effectively, as we shall see in the next chapter, it was a miracle.

Now, I would like you to listen to the voice of an actual witness to the Nazi crimes, P.O.W. No. 2406004, German Lieutenant Erwin Bingert[6]. Excerpts from his testimony illustrate German deceit and the cruelty of the Jewish "good neighbors," the Ukrainians. Hostile acts were widely perpetrated immediately after the Germans invaded Russian soil in 1941. The testimony was as follows:

"An order had been posted in the streets of Uman and...had been given the widest publicity throughout Uman sub-district by the Ukrainian Militia.... 'For the purpose of preparing an exact census of the Jewish population in the town of Uman, and in its sub-district, all Jews, of all ages, must appear on the day appointed hereunder at the respective places of registration. Persons failing to comply with the order will be punished most severely.'

"The result of this proclamation was, of course, that all persons concerned appeared as ordered. The relatively harmless summons, we thought, could be connected in some way or other with the preparations we were observing.

"... One row of Jews was ordered to move forward and was then allocated to the different tables where they had to undress completely and hand over everything they wore and carried. Some still carried jewelry, which they had to put on the table. Then, having taken off all their clothes, they were made to stand in line in front of the ditches, irrespective of their sex. The commandos then marched in behind the line and began to perform the inhuman acts, the horror of which is now known to the whole world.

"With automatic pistols and 0.8 pistols these men mowed down the line with such zealous intent that one could have supposed this activity to have been their life-work. Even women carrying children a fortnight to three weeks old, sucking at their breasts, were not spared this horrible ordeal. Nor were mothers spared the terrible sight of their children being gripped by their little legs and put to death by one stroke of the pistol-butt or club, thereafter to be thrown on the heap of human bodies in the ditch, some of whom were not quite dead. Not before these mothers had been exposed to this worst of all tortures did they receive the bullet that released them from this sight...

"...All this was so incomprehensible. How could a nation have the audacity to perpetrate, through its supreme leader and his Elite troops, acts such as these for which there could be no excuse under any circumstances?...

...I was given to understand that a special express order had been issued by Reichsfuehrer-SS Himmler, and personally signed by him. Upon request I was allowed to see this document. It read:

Soldiers of the Waffen-SS!

In the forest of Vinnitsa, District of Kiev, six of our best officers were found assassinated, hanging on a tree. The details are as follows: They were found naked with their legs pointing upwards, their bodies slit open and their intestines showing.

As a result of this case I have decided upon the following measures: As it may be taken for granted that this action was carried out by Jewish partisans, I hereby order that in the District of Kiev 10,000 Jews—irrespective of sex or age—are to die for each of the six officers mentioned above.

Even the child in the cradle must be trampled down like a poisonous toad. May each one of you be mindful of his oath and of his duty, whatever may be demanded of you.

We are living in an epoch of iron during which it is also necessary to sweep with iron-made brooms....

"...The Ukrainian SS-trained Militia was ordered to move into Uman. This body was again commanded by a small group of SS officers and N.C.O.'s. By this maneuver the events which were about to take place would assume a national Ukrainian character. This purpose was fully attained, as transcribed from the report carried by the so-called free Ukrainian press following the new 'action.'...

"...Ukrainian Militia, on horseback, armed with pistols, rifles, and long, straight cavalry swords, were riding wildly inside and around the town park. As far as we could make out, they were driving people along before their horses—men, women, and children. A shower of bullets was then fired at this human mass. Those not hit outright were struck down with the swords. Like some ghostly apparition, this horde of Ukrainians, led and let loose by SS officers, trampled savagely over human bodies, ruthlessly killing innocent children, mothers, and old people whose only crime was that they had escaped the great mass murder- -to be eventually beaten or shot to death like wild animals...."

Chapter VI

JEWISH RESISTANCE

In any reaction of a group to imminent danger the following factors decide the intensity of the response or lack of it: (a) the immediate situation, including the strength of the opposing forces, allies or foes, the terrain of action; (b) the cohesiveness of the group, manifested not only by group identity, its spirit, but also by past experience; (c) the individual conscience and social-psychological attitudes developed by education and cultural heritage; and (d) susceptibility to methods used by the enemy, including timing of repressive actions, physical terror, and propaganda. Only by knowing these factors can we know enough about a group's situation so as to judge its choices. For additional evaluation we might compare such criteria with the reactions of other groups in similar situations.

The first factor was discussed in the previous chapter. I concluded that, facing the criminal laws of the Nazi state, the Jews, robbed of their possessions, displaced, concentrated in a small area of the ghetto, surrounded by a population often more malicious than the Germans, without weapons or help from the Western Allies, found themselves in a most undesirable situation, incapable of resistance to Nazi destruction.

I started to develop the second factor (cohesiveness of the group), pointing out the strong family and community ties and the deep sense of responsibility for the prevention of harm to the group. The young and the daring had to restrain themselves and control their natural impulse toward a positive physical action, lest they jeopardize the existence of the others. They knew that their escape from the ghetto would bring retaliation against those remaining.

The third factor was also of great importance. Deeply religious, the majority trusted that God, Who had helped them throughout history, would not forsake them now. Psychologically, Jews were not geared to violence, having been brought up for centuries under the commandment "And thou shall love". This attitude, and past confrontations with stronger adversaries, had taught them that it is better to find a peaceful solution than to offer violent opposition.

According to the memoirs of Hersh Berlinski, referred to by Kubovy[1], Jewish leaders in the Warsaw ghetto in the second half of July 1942 expressed the belief in the providence of God. The leader of the orthodox party, Agudah Israel, Alexander Zysie Fridman said: "I believe in God and in a miracle. God will not permit his people, Israel, to be destroyed. We must wait and a miracle will certainly occur. There is no sense in fighting the Germans! They can finish us off in a few days, as happened in Lublin. But if matters drag on as they do now, this will take much time, and a miracle will occur". Jewish history (in fact, world history) knew no precedent to the approaching total annihilation, and Rabbi Fridman, like most of the Jews of that particular moment, believed that the resettlement was not wholesale murder and that only perhaps 60,000, but not all , Jews in the ghetto would be resettled.

Like others he opposed those who called for an immediate revolt, fearing that inevitably it would bring total disaster. The historian I.Schiper, who pointed out that in past history Jews had gained more by avoiding physical confrontation, supported Fridman at that meeting. He, too, could not foresee the unimaginable.

The great poet Itzhak Katznelson, killed the following year in Auschwitz, wrote at Camp Vittel in 1943 in his *Last Writings*: "They believed, the gentiles believed, but we, who were destined to be killed, we did not believe. Not a Jew believed what a vain nation, a fiendish breed, the dregs of impurity, could do, that it would set up a slaughterhouse for six million (perhaps far more, for there are no Jews left in Europe) for the entire Jewish people. Fortunate are we, for we did not believe because of God's image in us . . ."

The bearing of God's image in one's heart, the pacifistic attitude and love of one's fellow men were the cultural and religious brakes retarding Jewish resistance. The strength of the individual conscience found most accepting their deaths with dignity and nobility but could not protect their biological existence.

Kubovy describes this cultural characteristic of the Jewish people at a meeting of the World Jewish Congress in New York in 1942. Rabbis, when they were presented with suggestions to march on Washington and organize protest meetings, fiercely opposed such a program. "You are the gravediggers of our people," they said. "You have chosen to antagonize Hitler. You proclaimed a boycott against Germany. You published strongly worded resolutions. Hitler is not the first Haman in history. The experience of centuries has taught us how to deal with Haman. Stop your provocations. Let us rescue our people through our tested methods." [2] Great awareness of God's justice and protection made Jewish faith impervious to suspicion that the people faced genocide.

Hilberg's shameful accusation that the Jews became paralyzed after their first brush with death, in spite of advance knowledge of their fate, is at best an expression of his historical astigmatism and a severe confusion of facts.

Many individuals, defying the penalty of death for such deeds, supplied the starving ghetto with food obtained on the black market, smuggled in weapons, and carried important messages between camps. In order to organize actions against the Germans, the partisans needed help and information not available from the local population. A friend of mine who worked for the German military police, tried to obtain such intelligence.

Another example is the case of Daniel Rufeisen, better known as Brother Daniel. Presently a monk at the "Stella Maris" Monastery in Haifa, Rufeisen, once a member of the Zionist youth group, *Akiba*, first became a secretary to a police major in Mir. The Bielorussian police chief sponsored him for the advanced job as an assistant to the chief of the local Gestapo. Beginning as a translator, he became a NCO and took over responsibility for the storage and upkeep of arms. After he discovered the planned Gestapo "action" against local Bielorussians, he was able to warn them in time and so many lives were saved. Afterwards he contacted Jews from the local ghetto. He supplied them with a number of revolvers and guns. In due time he notified them about the pending action. As a result, three hundred Jews were able to save themselves. Of this group, the Russians killed one hundred eighty in the forest, the Germans captured twenty, and about one hundred survived.

Before the final showdown with the Nazis, such forms of resistance existed in every ghetto. Some of them, like the necessity of getting food from the black market, resulted from the need to sustain life. Jews could not live on the 184 calories per day allotted to them. Other forms, like smuggling weapons, show that the Jews prepared themselves to fight back at the risk of their lives.

The timing and secrecy of German "actions," plus the lack of weapons, fully explain the absence of a general uprising in the beginning of the deportations. The SS and their auxiliary units, heavily equipped, would descend suddenly under cover of night. The morning would find the ghetto completely encircled with no possibility of escape.

The action was swift, lasting only several hours. In one of Heydrich's reports to which Hilberg refers,[4] we read that shootings were carried out in such a manner that the population hardly noticed them.

The morning would find the ghetto completely encircled with no possibility of escape.

The action was swift, lasting only several hours. In one of Heydrich's reports to which Hilberg refers,[4] we read that shootings were carried out in such a manner that the population hardly noticed them. The inhabitants and even the survivors among the Jews had frequently been left with the impression that the victims had only been resettled.

Ringelblum writes that if the Jews had only had weapons (refused them by the Poles), they would have staged an armed resistance before the August, 1942 "actions" in spite of the fact that they did not know what their fate was going to be. *If* they had only known that death loomed for them, they would have fought even with fists and knives. Therefore, the historian's question as to why no instant revolt was staged finds its obvious answer: a tragedy which no one foresaw and which nobody believed possible had no need of being averted. This also answers the question raised by Joshua Perle[5] in his diary after the great action took place.

Thus, the fourth factor responsible for the Jewish behavior in the ghetto was probably the crucial one.

Even before the Jews found out about the true destination of the transports, as Hilberg says, on August 21, 1942, when the deportations were at their peak, the Jewish underground assassinated a number of policemen, informers and collaborators. They were people who not only lacked the Jewish individual conscience, but also should not be considered Jews. An example was the police chief, Jozef Szerynski, an apostate, known before the war for his anti-Jewish attitude. Obviously, Joshua Perle, who, on the 31st of August 1942, started. to write his diary, had no contact with the world or perhaps was in hiding, since at least one week after Szerynski's liquidation by the Jews, he complains that no one of the 300,000 ghetto dwellers had the courage to inflict punishment on at least one Jewish policeman.

Opposing the order in a totalitarian state is unthinkable for those who are not only excluded from participation in power but are even deprived of their most basic rights. If we comprehend this, we might easily understand the function of the Jewish police. The words of Rabbi Leo Baeck, the Jewish leader of Berlin, expressed this when he tried to explain his employment of Jewish policemen in rounding up Jews: "It would be better for them to do it, because they could at least be more gentle and helpful than the Gestapo and make the ordeal easier. It was scarcely in our power to oppose the order effectively."

In retrospect, one can easily understand the thoughts of Jews stricken with sadness, grief, and self-accusations for not having reacted in time. Joshua Perle wrote:

"It would have been possible to defend ourselves, not to let ourselves be slaughtered like so many stupid oxen. If all the Jews had left their houses, if they had broken through the walls (it would have been easy, too), if they had inundated all the streets of Warsaw like a flood, with shouting, with axes, with stones, with meat-choppers, they might have shot ten thousand of us, perhaps twenty thousand. But they would not have been able to kill three times a hundred thousand people. We might have died then too, but we would have died with a bit of honor. Those who would have remained alive would have spread out over the entire land, in all the little towns and villages. It would not have been an easy task for the murderers to kill us all."[6]

It is hard to understand the psychology of the few European refugees who distort the truth, who, instead of feeling compassion for those who perished, while they were fortunate to be living in the USA during World War II, criticize them. By distorting the facts, they bring shame to the name of Jews, as much as do the ghetto policemen whom they condemn. Because of the misrepresentations of the Jewish defense effort, their books became food for anti-Jewish propaganda.

Yuri Suhl, whose book *They Fought Back*[7] should be known to everybody who is interested in the story of the Jewish resistance, exposes, for example, Hilberg's misleading information.

The Warsaw ghetto resistance lasted longer than the 1939 campaign in Poland and the 1940 campaign in France. It was the first large-scale battle of the civilian population against Nazi terror. Even the Nazis, in their reports, recognized the heroism of those defenders who "preferred to fling themselves to the flames rather than surrender...." What was unusual was the disproportionate relationship of numbers, equipment, and military skill of the opposing forces.

In reporting final losses, Hilberg, though familiar with other sources, chose to use Stroop's report--16 dead and 85 wounded on the German side, including collaborators. If he was basing his information on the Nazi Brigadefuehrer responsible for the destruction of the ghetto, he could at least have mentioned the other two known sources: the newspaper *Glos Warszawy*, reporting about 360 dead and over 1,000 wounded as the German casualties during the first week alone. There also exists a telegram from the leaders of the Jewish underground to Dr. Schwartzbart in London indicating German losses for the first nine days as 1,000 dead and wounded. In their message the Jews let the world know that theirs was a heroism of which they were fully conscious: "The heroic rising without precedent in history, of the doomed sons of the ghetto, should at least awaken the world to deeds commensurate with the gravity of the hour." But the world remained silent, and no help came—neither from the Poles nor from the Allied Powers—to those who, often with bare hands, fought tanks, flame throwers, and airplanes.

In Bialystok during the ghetto revolt the notorious murderer, S.S. Major General Odilo Globocnik, resorted to tanks, armored cars, and airplanes. The Jews defended themselves for four days. But Hilberg describes it differently. In Bialystok, he informs us, on August 15, 1943 there was scattered fighting for about twenty-four hours. Hilberg mentions that in Vilna the Jewish resistance fought a small and unsuccessful battle with the Germans invading the ghetto during the closing days. He also prefers to omit the blowing up of a military train by Jewish youths in May of 1942, which resulted in the death of 200 soldiers, the wounding of many others, and the damage of military equipment.

Writing about the revolt in the Sobibor extermination camp, Hilberg described it in three sentences, and, says Suhl, he misrepresented the facts in two of them. Instead of the 150 inmates, as reported by Hilberg, there were actually 600 who made a break for freedom. About 400 succeeded. Afterwards, half fell as casualties of land mines or of those in pursuit. According to Thomas Blatt, 49 escapees finally made it to freedom. He was one of them. Instead of one SS-man killed, as reported by Hilberg, there were ten SS killed, one wounded, and thirty-eight Ukrainian guards killed or wounded.

Aryeh Kubovy,[8] among others, has lashed out forcefully at Bruno Bettelheim and Hannah Arendt, claiming that they have both vilified the murdered Jewish people; that Bettelheim, who publicly defended Arendt, was the first to rob them of the respect due to their memory and the tragic fate they suffered. In 1960, in his book, *The Informed Heart*, Bettelheim wrote that millions of European Jews who did not escape in time or could not go underground could at least have marched as free men against the SS, rather than wait to be rounded up and walk to the gas chambers. Both, Bettelheim and Arendt strongly criticize the victims and only have sympathy for the misunderstood murderers. According to their thesis, the dehumanization of man in a totalitarian regime affects persecutors and their victims alike, and any cooperation with such a regime must lead to both the disintegration of the personality and to extermination. This hindsight wisdom deprives the Jewish victims of respect. Pointing out their inability to grasp the dangers that confronted them, one indirectly says that they were not very smart!

I have already stressed the importance of the propaganda aimed toward the spiritual shattering of the Jews, the loss of their traditional sharp distinction between what is ethical and what is criminal. I mentioned that the Jews never lost this essence of their spiritual existence, except for an insignificant number of those on the fringes of Judaism. Those who try to bridge the moral gap between the Nazis and their victims fall into this small category; they have been conquered by Nazi propaganda.

We know that during the great "actions" in 1942, between 70 and 85% of European Jewry perished thinking only that they were being "resettled," not suspecting even the existence of concentration camps. Bettelheim wanted them to march as free men against the SS. Why did he not show that courage when they dragged him to the camps in Dachau and Buchenwald? Why did Arendt, at that time still a young woman, not try to do what Hannah Senesch did? (H. Senesch was one of thirty-two volunteer parachutists sent behind the German lines to carry on rescue activities among their fellow Jews.) Both of these Jews derided other Jews as an expression of self-hatred.

Some names in the Jewish resistance became famous—like those of Dr. Atlas or Bielski; thousands remained unknown. Thousands of others appear in the literature as members of the national group with which they united to fight the enemy. Yehiel Granatstein and Moshe Kahanovich undertook to identify those Jewish partisans considered to be Poles, Russians or French Maquis in *Lexicon Hagevurah*[9].

We must understand that a man, stripped of clothes, terrorized and bare-handed facing machinegun barrels, can use but little physical force to defend himself. This applies to hundreds of Poles on German liquidation lists, to the victims of Lidice in Czechoslovakia, those of Oradur-sur-Glane in France, and those of many other places. Not only civilians—women and children--behaved the way they did, but also men trained to resist, such as the Russian POWs, American POWs in Malmedy in Belgium, and German POWs during the initial "orgy" of the victorious Russians in 1945.

The calmness and dignity with which Jews faced death has been described even by their enemies. It was not due to indifference, as the Germans wanted to believe, for the Jews love life, but it was due to an unshakable strength gained from their belief in God and in ultimate justice.

The true democrats, especially in the United States appreciated the heroic attitude of the Jewish victims, especially those, who resisted the barbarian Nazis.

The following are some contributions to the observance of the Twentieth Anniversary of the Warsaw Ghetto Uprising. They illustrate the determination and spiritual survival of the Jewish people in the aftermath of incredibly harsh harassment, persecution and deprivation:

Senator Kenneth Keating- -

"Mr President,

In April 1943 the Jewish inhabitants of the Warsaw ghetto rose in rebellion against the tyranny of Nazi rule. In an epic struggle of incredible valor, the people of the Warsaw ghetto defied the armed might of Nazi military power, and gave to the entire world an example of courage and self-sacrifice that has never been equaled. Although the valiant freedom fighters of the ghetto well knew that they were hopelessly outnumbered and that they alone could never succeed in bringing down Hitler's military power, their rebellion was a triumphant reaffirmation of the eternal striving of all mankind for freedom, dignity, and spiritual independence. Faith and religious dedication filled them; and with the bravery of desperation they were able to inflict substantial setbacks on the Nazi army.

Mr. President, I am proud to have been the author of Senate Joint Resolution 179, which was passed by the Congress of the United States in August 1962, and was signed by the President on August 28, 1962. This resolution rightly called the attention of the country to the 20th anniversary of this tragic uprising, and specifically called upon the President to issue a proclamation for the observance of April 21 as Warsaw Ghetto Day with appropriate ceremonies and activities...."[10]

Senator Clifford Case:

"Mr. President, 20 years ago, from April 19 to May 8, 1943 the Jew of the Warsaw ghetto carried on a heroic and hopeless fight against the overwhelming power of the Nazi troops bent on their extermination.

While each of us would probably rather forget that humanity is capable of acts of extermination such as those carried on by the Nazis, I think it is well for us to look back on this tragic event, perhaps the most tragic event in recent history. For a new generation has grown up since 1943 which might otherwise never fully realize that acts such as this took place during their childhood.

Reflection on the Warsaw uprising will remind us, too, of the valor of the human spirit, as well as the need to prevent any recurrence of the depravity of which man is also capable. With a little sharper awareness of the danger of mass murder, our country might long since have ratified the Genocide Convention, signed by our Government at the United Nations in 1948....[11]

The Warsaw Ghetto Uprising—A Proclamation by the President of the United States of America

The White House, March 5, 1963:

"Of the more than 400,000 Jews whom the Nazis had previously walled into the Warsaw ghetto, only about 70,000 remained in April of 1943. With deadly efficiency, most of the other inhabitants had been transported by the Nazis to concentration camps and had there been exterminated. The surviving Jews, suffering from malnutrition and disease, with pitifully few weapons and virtually no hope of assistance from any source, determined to sell their lives as dearly as possible. They engaged the Nazis in battle.

The result was known by the Jews to be foredoomed.

Yet, though they lacked both military resources and a military tradition, they were able to conduct their struggle against the overwhelming forces of the Nazi occupiers for more than 3 weeks. Thereby they provided a chapter in the annals of human heroism, an inspiration to the peace-loving people of the world, and a warning to would-be oppressors which will long be remembered.

Now, therefore, I, John F. Kennedy, President of the United States of America, in consonance with the joint resolution of Congress approved August 28, 1962 (76 Stat. 407); do hereby invite the people of the United States to observe the 20th anniversary of the Warsaw ghetto uprising, April 21, 1963, with appropriate ceremonies and activities.

In witness whereof, I have hereunto set my hand and caused the seal of the United States of America to be affixed.

Done at the city of Washington this 4th day of March in the year of our Lord 1963, and the independence of the United States the 187th.

(seal)   John F. Kennedy

By the President:

Dean Rusk, Secretary of State[12]

Senator Jacob K. Javits-: "I would consider it a privilege to include my views reflecting the extraordinary courage and heroism of the Jews of Warsaw in their resistance to the Nazis with those of other representative leaders in government, religion, education, and the art.

The memory of the 50,000 men, women and children who fought against overwhelming odds, under hopeless conditions and in certainty of death, continues to live in the hearts and the minds of all mankind. The act of resistance immortalized these martyrs of the Warsaw Ghetto as the personification of human dignity, certain of their mission in history and their place as Jews. For more than a month they carried on a desperate organized resistance against the full might of Nazi tanks, guns and gas. They fought from the first day of the Passover until the middle of May, and a few last-ditch survivors continued to fight amidst the rubble until the end of September, 1943. They left reports, diaries, letters and other accounts of their last days, eyewitness materials that have inscribed forever the greatness as well as the shame of which human beings and children in the Warsaw Ghetto were despised and degraded. In death they won a great victory.[13]

Mayor of New York, John V. Lindsay:

This year the Jews of the world are mourning the victims of the Warsaw Ghetto. Memorial services are being held in synagogues in Berlin and London and New York, as well as in Israel and Warsaw itself. For, the forty thousand who died in the Warsaw Ghetto were Jews, and they died because they were Jews. But be-fore these men and women were Jews, before they were Poles, they were human beings. And they were destroyed, not by bullets or shells or fire, but by other human beings.

The tragedy of the uprising in the Warsaw Ghetto was not merely a tragedy for the Jewish people; it was a tragedy for the whole human race, for Jews and non-Jews alike. The Jews of the world are mourning this year; the whole world should mourn. "Never send to ask for whom the bell tolls, it tolls for thee." [14]

Senator Everett N. Dirksen : "April 21, 1963 having been designated by the United States Senate and proclaimed by President Kennedy as the 20th anniversary commemorating the uprising of the Jews of the Warsaw Ghetto against the Nazis, it is fitting and proper that the world be reminded of these atrocities and brutal extermination of innocent people by the Nazis, and a warning to dictators that atrocities such as these will not be tolerated by a civilized world. Taking a quotation from President Abraham Lincoln's Gettysburg Address, which is quite apropos, I would like to repeat, "The world will little note, nor long remember what we say here, but it can never forget what they did here. It is for us the living, rather, to be dedicated here to the unfinished work which they who fought here have thus far so nobly advanced." [15]

Senator Clair Engle:..."It is in the interest of a permanent world peace that we do not forget the brutal atrocities of the Nazis and that we keep alive for the new generations the story of the indomitable spirit of the Warsaw Jews.

As President Kennedy has said, the nameless Ghetto fighters provided "a chapter in the annals of human heroism, an inspiration to the peace-loving people of the world and a warning to would-be oppressors." [16]

Chapter VII

THE GERMAN RESISTANCE

Commenting on the failure of the attempt to kill Hitler, Shirer[1], refers to Guderian, whom he quotes: "At that time-- the fact seems beyond dispute-- the great proportion of the German people still believed in Adolf Hitler and would have been convinced that with his death the assassin had removed the only man who might still have been able to bring the war to a favorable conclusion." Shirer also repeats General Blumentritt's opinion that "one-half of the civil population was shocked that the German generals had taken part in the attempt to overthrow Hitler, and felt bitterly toward them in consequence- -and the same feeling was manifested in the Army itself." In spite of the late hour of the revolt, knowledge of the turning tide of the war, and all the atrocities committed by the Nazis, the majority of the Germans persevered in their unflagging allegiance to Hitler. As Shirer says, they followed him blindly, like dumb cattle, differing from the animal herd only in faith and enthusiasm.

Though some of the objectives of the German conspirators were aimed at the social and racial injustices of the Third Reich, only a few stressed the fact that the persecution of the Jews was one of the main motives for their resistance. There were those who, like Moltke and von Wartenburg, belonged to the "Kreisau Circle" and could not see nationalism without humanitarianism. Others, like Leber, Mierendorf and Reichwein felt that social justice was incompatible with anti-Judaism. Most Germans in the resistance believed that only the inhumane persecution of Jews should have been abolished simply because it depraved the German character and set the world's opinion against Germany. They were not totally dedicated to the rejection of the racial theory and to the restoration of equal rights to the Jews.

Compared to the participants in ghetto and concentration camp uprisings, there is no doubt that the German resistance had chances of success immeasurably greater than they had, and still it failed. Members of the resistance, unlike Jews, were free people who could travel not only in Germany but also abroad, where they had contact with representatives of the Western Powers. The Jews had no help and no freedom of movement. German conspirators came from the top of the social pyramid: they were known generals, aristocrats, and clergymen—people who exercised authority or power. The Jews were outside of human society. Only a few German revolutionaries of that time came from the masses—for example, those in the student revolt in Munich, 1943. Those who could bring the resistance a promise of success came only from the military brass, including even the popular Field Marshall Erwin Rommel[2]. The partially successful coup of July 20, 1944 by Count Klaus von Stauffenberg resulted in minor interference with the Nazi machine and in complete disaster for the resistance.

We do know that Carl Goerdeler, the mayor of Leipzig, and Karl Stroelin, the mayor of Stuttgart, dared to demand from the Ministry of the Interior in 1943 a system of justice free of the SS terror with no persecution of Jews and churches. Though a Nazi, Generalkommissar Wilhelm Kube opposed the barbaric and sadistic treatment of Jews by the SS in *Ostland*.

Those Germans who let the world know about Nazi crimes deserve as much of our admiration as their brothers who attempted armed resistance. There was Kurt Gerstein, the famous SS man who, out of deep religious or at least ethical convictions, enrolled in this military organization in order to be able to unmask its secrets. Unfortunately, in the course of his activities he became instrumental in the Zyklon B killings at Belzec, but all evidence indicates that he was pressured to do this against his convictions, and that he tried to stop it through outside intervention, especially that of the Pope, who remained silent.

There were Germans who helped Jews at the risk of their lives, and these were inscribed in the eternal book of Jewish "Righteous Men," somewhat corresponding to the Christian saints. One such man was Sergeant of the Wehrmacht Anton Schmidt who helped the Jewish underground in Vilna He brought Jews from that city in trucks to Bialystok. He hid Jews in his house. He was arrested and killed for aiding Jews.

We can see that even within the existing framework of Nazi totalitarianism Germans could have shown more humanitarianism—as some of them with individual consciences did. To be willing to use one's individual conscience in those times was synonymous with a revolt. And revolt led, almost inevitably, to death.

Chapter VIII

CRIME AND FORGIVENESS

To ask forgiveness from the close relatives of those who were so cruelly annihilated by cold, premeditated, systematic methods is sheer perfidy. It is equivalent to drawing them into the orbit of active participation, neutralizing the abysmal loss and suffering. It is demanding that Christian conscience in general and German in particular is purified with the soap made out of Jewish bodies. To ease the conscience of the killer who has repeated his acts during the same generation and in each generation for the last seventeen hundred years means to cooperate with him, to let him achieve, by appeal to pity, that which he was unable to change by fire, sword, and crematoria. To give up resentment against the criminal means the total change of our values and diminution of the scope of the crime. This would make the crime itself insignificant, and we would abandon our concept of justice, which is the cornerstone of our belief. If madmen committed this sacrifice of European Jewry, their asking the survivors for forgiveness is a continuation of that detachment from reality. These crimes cannot be forgiven. No one has the right of forgiveness for the loss of six million innocent lives.

These crimes were not only committed in cold blood, but also in the name of an unconventional morality, pulling mankind's conscience from Mount Sinai to Auschwitz. In his speech to the Gruppenfuehrer in Poznan, October 4, 1943, Himmler said that the SS men had the *moral* right vis-a-vis the ethics of their own people to annihilate the Jewish people. Forgiveness, now, would mean sanctioning such a morality. Whatever compassion was still left for the Jews in Christian hearts was condemned, and conscience, called by Hitler "a Jewish invention, " disappeared. All humane instincts were stilled. Himmler termed the killing of a million Jewish children "decent" and "a page of glory in German history." After subjecting all Europe to a bloodbath, Hitler called the innocent Jews, killed by him, the real criminals. He described their death as atonement for their guilt.

I would not give absolution to a people who pillaged, destroyed, burned books and distorted truth, starved their victims and supported the biological "Final Solution" along with the Jewish spirit of justice. That spirit is still alive in the ashes of Auschwitz and Majdanek. I do not bargain daily with my God to forgive me my sins as I forgive those who sinned against me. My belief is rational and not based on mystic contradictions with reality. My stand is crystal clear: no forgiveness. If there is a reversal of societal consciousness, it is of a mild degree, even without a general educational program, and therefore, without merits of change of morals.

There can be no hesitation in this decision, not one angstrom, particularly, in the presence of tolerance shown for neo-Nazism and for historical revisionism, which is denying the history of the Holocaust.

There can be no forgiveness of Hitler or of the Nazis. This was their "final solution" to the ethical, religious, and physical uprooting of an innocent people, started as early as the second century, AD At that time the Church usurped names identifying Jews, calling them the Temple of Satan, and considering itself the true Israel. The Christian beliefs withdrew from the Jewish teachings of Jesus of love and kindness, to an unrecognizable distance: from justice here and now to salvation in the hereafter, from one's own contribution to build the Kingdom of God, to the sacrifice of somebody else who is dying for your sins, from giving to receiving. Human sacrifices are considered an utmost abomination by the Torah and had already been rejected by Abraham, who went through the motions, but refused to sacrifice his son Isaac. The prophets, Isaiah and Micah said that God does not want animal sacrifices either. We know nothing about the hereafter. Rabbi Jacob said (*Ethics of the Fathers*): "better is one hour of repentance and good deeds in this world than the entire life of the world to come".

The missionary zeal of the Christians forced salvation on the Jews when all they wanted was to stay alive. The Christians burned them alive. I still see the graves, into which the Jews were thrown, moving for hours. The Holocaust was just the last act of a drama which began in the times of the early Christian fathers.

The recent discoveries of the historical Jesus, a Jewish patriot and teacher of social justice, and of those responsible for His death, brought sobering thoughts to some theologians, but are denounced by the organized Church, which would not among other things, like to assume the important culpability for paving the road to the Holocaust with its false teachings. Those missionaries who diligently work to convince Jews to accept their religious system, whose historical and philosophical foundations crumble, of course, dislike the truth. These new historical insights into the origins of Christianity are stunning.

Therefore, people like Robert Funk, head of the controversial Jesus Seminar, which concluded that no more than 20 percent of sayings and even fewer of the deeds attributed in the Gospels to Jesus are authentic, are considered a threat to existing Christian beliefs. Funk told a group of people that modern Christians "can no longer swallow the kind of mythology that has dominated the faith for the past 2,000 years." (U.S. News & World Report, August 4, 1997).

John Dominic Crossan, a biblical scholar, in his book "The Historical Jesus: The Life of a Mediterranean Jewish Peasant" does not believe that most of the stories from the New Testament have historical roots. He insists that only the Romans were responsible for the death of Jesus. This ipso facto clears Jews, who were accused for all those centuries, as Christ-killers.

Christians themselves now challenge the basic Christian beliefs. Some of the Christian philosophers do not believe in the bodily resurrection of Jesus, others-in the life after death. The Torah doesn't mention life after death, but for Christians, the salvation in the hereafter is essential. Christ's resurrection, an essential belief of Christians, has been denied and called "an embarrassment to the modern mind and a disservice to the itinerant Jewish preacher from rural Galilee.... Liberal scholars who think the time has come to replace the "cultic" Jesus of Christian worship with the "real" Jesus unearthed by academic research."

Kai Nielsen wrote in "The Faces of Immortality": 'Conceptions of the afterlife are so problematical that it is unreasonable for a philosophical and scientifically sophisticated person living in the West in the Twentieth Century to believe in life eternal, to believe that we shall survive the rotting or the burning or the mummification of our present bodies'. (Philosophy of Religion Conference, January 30, 1987 Death and Afterlife, Claremont Graduate School)

I asked one of the most prominent theologians: What is left of Christian beliefs, after finding the historical Jesus, after discarding the myth of the immaculate conception of the Virgin Mary on one hand, and plans to create a new, controversial dogma, that she is a Co-Redeemer, after disbelief in the afterlife, and of a few other basic concepts? His answer was: "tradition", with its love-hate relationship to the mother religion, Judaism. Many theologians keep their religious beliefs separated from the historical clarity of new discoveries, and therefore frequently they do not believe what they preach.

Times have changed. The post-war years which ushered in a new era of ecumenism brought an understanding of the injustices perpetrated on the Jews in the name of religion. Is there not a need for much stronger condemnation of the past teachings of contempt for Jews? It is morally wrong not to admit who led the teachings, who organized the Crusades, who blessed the fascists artillery, who, surrounded by pontifical splendor and with the greatest spiritual power on earth, condoned or incited persecutions, and did not utter a single word in sparing the Jews? Why, knowing the truth, does the same Church not announce loudly, "*urbi et orbi*", that she contributed to the destruction of a people with her false doctrine? Why does she not reveal the truth to every Christian in every city, in every village, in every Church? How can she, invoking God, not admit the guilt of false accusation for the death of Jesus, who was charged with preparing a revolt against Rome, and for her role in preparing the death of millions of His brothers and sisters?

Jews certainly are more preoccupied than Christians are, with their losses and persecutions. Still, they have the right to demand (as a precondition to a dialogue) that there be an admission of guilt not only from knowledgeable theologians but also in the heart and mind of every Christian. That is not too much to ask.

The second Vatican Council brought some thawing in Christian-Jewish relationships. The blood of the Holocaust reflected not only the nadir of premeditated and repeated cruelties, but also the catastrophic crisis of Christian ethics and morals. Not because of love or compassion for them were the Jews magnanimously cleared of a sin they had not committed, but because of the voices of the Schweitzers and Hochhuths. These men could no longer separate themselves from the admission of guilt on the part of the Church, and from revealing the inhumanity in those who supposedly represent God on earth. The Church hierarchy, including Pope Paul, did its utmost to hush those voices of conscience. They pointed to the fact that single Jews were hidden by Pius XII in Castel Gandolfo. Granted, but some Jewish individuals were also spared by Eichmann and Himmler. In general, what was the attitude of each of these individuals?

Pius XII, still the greatest exponent of spiritual authority in Europe, chose not to speak out in behalf of the Jews. Sapieha of Poland frequently reported the facts to him in detail, as did Orsenigo of Berlin, and Donati of France. In his general expressions on the horrors of war, not once did he condemn persecutions of the Jews. Supposedly, he remained silent so as to prevent "worse things." Obviously, if he knew that their total annihilation was unavoidable without external intervention, and if he decided not to intervene, the only worse thing that could happen would be "the survival of the Jews." Couldn't one perhaps draw the conclusion that Pius XII was glad for the opportunity to have Nazi Germany do the "dirty work" in getting rid of the religious opposition which the Church was never able to destroy? Some have arrived at such conclusions. It took over 50 years for the Catholic Church in France to atone for its silence during the killing of French Jews, not only under pressure of the German Nazis, but of the initiative of Frenchmen under the leadership of their own Marshal Petain.

Although Rolf Hochhuth shocked the Christian world with his denunciation of the Church and of Pius XII in his book, *The Deputy* [1], the Jews knew all along that the Vatican had not shown any concern for their Calvary. It was nothing new to them. Still, when Pope John XXIII showed the Jews his human heart and began to work to stop the traditional hostility towards them, their appreciation was without limits.

After discussing the guilt of those responsible for the Holocaust, I would like to analyze briefly their feeling of culpability for it. Freud's definition of guilt is relevant here. He saw the sense of guilt born from the tension between the super-ego and the subordinate ego. This tension (lack of psychological balance) results in the need for punishment.

When values were changed, as in Nazi Germany, the super-ego was altered by the philosophy of the robots, individual conscience disappeared, and the above mentioned tension and sense of guilt ceased to exist. People of this type do not feel the normal need for punishment for their unethical conduct, nor do they need forgiveness. This was the case of the majority of Germans under the Nazi regime. Those few who preserved their individual conscience, their super-ego, and acted in an ethical way, do not share guilt with the rest.

Most of those who are asking for forgiveness did not participate in the horrors of the Holocaust at all: clergymen, housewives, students, and children of the guilty generation. They feel guilty not for personal transgressions but as members of a nation which perpetrated those crimes. There is also a feeling of guilt among some Christians outside Germany for standing by and not helping the victims, and also for belonging to a church, the teachings of which were indirectly responsible for the Holocaust. These people are even less involved in the criminal acts than the innocent Germans were, yet theirs is also the guilt of a member of an involved group. In a sense, we are all members of the same group, and we are all involved.

A German asked me: "How can we improve without forgiveness?" I answered him by quoting the New Testament:

"Woe unto the world because of offences...Woe to that man by whom the offence comes" (Matthew 18:7). And we read further (Matthew 18:21-22): "Then came Peter to him and said, Lord, how often shall my brother sin against me, and I forgive him? till seven times? Jesus said to him, I do not say to you, until seven times: but until seventy-seven times." Jesus did not say six million times. We all recognize the need of redemption and for forgiveness. We cannot turn our backs and walk away saying: "You created a Frankenstein in your souls, now you have to live with him". We cannot tolerate a Frankenstein in the hearts of people who can destroy the earth. We must find a solution, perhaps without ever forgiving the guilty.

According to Jewish teaching, the sin can be redeemed through the initiative of the individual: Repentance, Prayer, and Good Deeds. However, in order to repent, the supplicant must first be aware of his transgression. He must face the truth by learning facts and actions, and recognize the degree of their deviation from ethical standards, and from God's law, as reflected in his individual conscience.

Thus, the study and teaching about concentration camps, Nazi atrocities, and the annihilation of European Jewry must replace the complete void of information in history books. There should be no more leaving out of this subject in discussions, especially with children, or sweeping it under the rug of the sub-conscious. This applies to the Gentile and. to the Jew alike. The latter, running away from the subject instead of facing it, will get lost in the labyrinth of guilt. After the supplicant has measured the degree of deviation from God's law and sincerely regrets that it occurred, he expresses a strong desire to correct it. If he believes in God, he appeals to Him for help; otherwise he invokes all the power of his super-ego in the decision to correct what is still correctable, or to compensate for that which is not correctable by good deeds. However these two phases of the effort to receive redemption, repentance and prayer, are of little significance in cases such as the Holocaust, where extinct lives cannot be restored. Only incessant involvement in the third phase toward obtaining redemption—compensation by good deeds—will bring the supplicant closer to his goal.

To summarize: the burden of the immeasurable guilt for the Holocaust cannot be relieved by human forgiveness. The individuals who took an active part in the Holocaust sloughed off their individual consciences and so they do not feel guilty; the few who obeyed their own conscience, committed no transgressions and also do not feel individually guilty. The guilt is a collective one. All are involved in it. In other words, the guilt does not involve the non-participants in the Holocaust other than as members of the Church, members of the German nation, or of the Western Democracies, which showed indifference or complicity with the Nazis. These institutions are guilty by directly or indirectly bringing about the catastrophe. Through Repentance, Prayer (theological or psychological), and Good Deeds the redemption can be achieved.

I wish to stress the fact that there is no "statute of limitations" on the burden of guilt. Legal justice may not be able to catch up with the culprit, may be blind or lenient, speedy or slow, or may be satisfied with the punishment or with absolving of the accused. It is not so with the individual conscience and the burden of guilt. They will haunt one "till the third and fourth generation" unless the process of redemption is successfully completed.

As mentioned before, repentance and prayer alone have no significance in achieving redemption unless they are accompanied by good deeds. Christian teaching differs from this view, for it is written (*Romans 3:28*): "Therefore we conclude that a man is justified by faith without the deeds of the law." In the condemnation of the guilty act there is a basic difference between the Christian teaching of collective responsibility for sin, a generalization that eventually led to the horrors of the Holocaust, and the Jewish precept of individual responsibility. The Church fathers condemned not only all contemporary Jews for their alleged participation in Jesus' death, but also all Jews of the future. We read in the New Testament (*Romans*: 19-19): "Therefore by the offence of one judgment came upon all men to condemnation; even so by the righteousness of one the free gift came upon all men unto justification of life. For as by one man's disobedience many were made sinners, so by the obedience of one shall many be made righteous."

The Jewish stand on individual responsibility is expressed by the following verse from the Torah: "The fathers shall not be put to death for the children, neither shall the children be put to death for the fathers; every man shall be put to death for his own sin" (Deuteronomy 24:16).

When I switched the discussion from guilty behavior to the feeling of guilt, it was noted that the latter depends on individual conscience and yet also appears as a collective phenomenon. Though individually not guilty, post-Nazi Germans of this generation still have a feeling of culpability for the crimes of their fathers. They show an awakening of individual conscience which, if it should last, could become the spark to kindle the flame of universal love. If indeed this young generation will bring about the brotherhood of men by constant conscientious effort, they will actually identify themselves with the ideals of the perished Jews, and, being conquered by those ideals, they will achieve redemption.

The feeling of guilt is now being compensated. In this case the "punishment" will be accomplished by replacing the Nazi ideas with the universal idea of Judaism, the brotherhood of all men. Christians know that union with the sacrifice of the Redeemer contributes to the reconstruction of the body of Christ (according to Pope Paul VI). Identification with the ideals of sacrificed Jews will contribute to the preservation of the essence of their existence, their spirituality and beliefs. In the encyclical *"Populorum progressio"*[2] we read, for example, that there must be a worldwide solidarity of people, and that all should help each other. Now, after the repentance and prayer, must come the good deeds. The young German generation will punish their fathers by showing them that there is a universal love, and individual conscience, and a feeling of guilt.

Well known is Hitler's saying: *"Das Gewissen, diese Judische Erfindung . . ."* (conscience, this Jewish invention...). If this "Jewish invention" will reign in human hearts, then the Holocaust was not completely in vain. Says a German writer[3] : "Auschwitz just removed our blindfolds and let us see... The first thing to do now after Auschwitz, before the relation between Christians and Jews can change basically and forever, is to express, by the younger brother, the supplication for forgiveness." Those young Germans who have recognized the light of human love are in a minority, but they have sincerity and a depth of affection, rarely seen. Their road to redemption is often undertaken with prayer. Such a prayer of the Pax-Christi group in Hamburg, presented by Gisela Wiese[4], follows:

"Our epoch is in Your hands, 0 Lord. What do 30 years mean for You! But we live in the days, as if the suffering of our Jewish brothers caused by our nation on 9 November 1938 had never occurred. You are being affected wherever men are beaten. Our nation let people follow Your road of Crucifixion, our nation let you suffer again. We can truly proclaim Your death and participate in Your resurrection only if we remember also the suffering and dying of these Your brothers and sisters. We recall the crashing of the window glass of that 9 November 1938, the screaming and the beating. We also turned away from You, O Lord. We recall how our Jewish co-citizens disappeared-how the residences were abandoned and the homes were left empty. Today we know more about their suffering and dying. We know about the Jewish mother who, dying, begged for the life of her small child and had to watch as it was murdered in front of her. We know about the woman physician who exclaimed at the hanging of her patients: "How do you want, you Germans, to meet with your God?"

We know that in the face of flames the faith of many was also consumed. We know about the terror which destroyed people, when they had to experience what one man is able to do to another.

Lord we take refuge with You. We want nothing to forget, nothing to evade, otherwise we would be more guilty than before....

We bring our request: Permit us today to see and act in Your love.

Men are again being deprived of their rights, persecuted, starved and tortured.,

We want to help to heal Your world. Help us in it, O Lord!"

The above prayer gives ample proof that in some of the Germans the awakening of the individual conscience is very real. Who would dare to consider them guilty of the cruelty of their fathers?

Chapter IX

TOWARD THE FUTURE AND NEW PERCEPTION OF GOD

We cannot bypass the Holocaust unperturbed and return to "business as usual." The Holocaust was the greatest tragedy that ever befell the Jewish people, or any people. It resulted from the death of individual conscience at a time preceding the latest technological revolution. During the biblical days prophets came forth to awaken the masses, to restore their moral obligations, to call for repentance and compensation for past transgressions in order to avoid punishment. Scientists are the prophets of today. They are much more advanced in predicting the future. They are able to calculate precisely the date and extent of doomsday. The recognition of the rapidly approaching danger, in which the scientist might be of more use than the prophet, is not enough. There has to be a will, a motivation to prevent it. Here is where the scientist lags behind the prophet, who knows how to restore individual conscience so that man cares, that he takes the initiative into his hands, starting from himself, from a change in his own attitude toward the world.

And simply because the predicted crisis might be the last one—and not for an isolated group of people, like, for example, the Jews in the past—but for all life on earth, there will be no surviving "master race," no tacit bystanders. All will be victims. There will be no guilt and forgiveness; the earth will be blasted back to the first day of Genesis when the human spirit was not yet projected and the "earth was *tohu va'vohu*, (unformed and void) and.. the Spirit of God hovered over the face of the waters."

With small exceptions, people lost their individual conscience during World War II—a loss labeled as the Death of God. They lost also sensitivity for history, care for others, and even for themselves-and they labeled it the Death of History. There is no doubt in the existence of History and of God, but there is little doubt in the spiritual Death of Mankind. This will determine Death of the Future. In order to avert this, man must eliminate from his intellectual armory these two deadly ideas: the Death of God, reflected in individual conscience, and the Death of History, reflected in our motivation to care and be involved in implementing justice.

Men must turn their eyes to the Holocaust. The Holocaust could be the greatest, and let us hope the last, lesson for the young generation. The young are right when they refuse to trust the older generation—the generation of World War II, which was responsible for the Holocaust, for the Death of God and History. Indeed, the young are right when they turn their backs on the politicians, on the churches and synagogues represented by hypocrites. The consecrated walls cannot replace the living human conscience. The young feared that perhaps they would never reach old age when they heard words like those written by the minister of defense of the USSR, Marshal Grechko: "The Americans are fooling themselves. The only war to fight, to win, is an atomic one, and that is what we shall be prepared for." [1]

The idea of God has faded in the hearts of those who live in a free society, but it was killed long ago in the land of the KGB, concentration camps, and mental wards. Our young people should be aware of the fact that by destroying the system of free expression, they will create a situation in which there is no hope, and no dialogue possible. They must preserve freedom. They should return to the churches and the synagogues and resurrect the human conscience. They must search for God; this will be their God, a new one, not inherited and distorted, not the one that is supposed to help in the exploitation of others, not the one who forsook beaten slaves and children burned in Auschwitz.

Let them find God, who is the source of justice, whom a man with individual conscience does not have to beg, but whom he worships by prayers, songs, love, and primarily by good deeds. Let them not shy away from politics; let them become involved in the exploitation of new scientific discoveries and direct them to good ends.

The young people don't have enough time to destroy the present system and build a new one—neither here, in a free society, or in the totalitarian countries. Young people have to get involved not through destruction, but by building new values. If these new builders become numerous enough—and they will, for the World War II generation will not live forever—they can effect radical changes. The young generation must find its own identity in a hurry. It is not enough to reject the traditional ties with the old generation—to rebel, to destroy, to run away helplessly from reality into the world of drugs, or to commit suicide. This reaction could be understood as the first attempt at severing ties with the values of the World War II generation, but if it persists, it can lead only to self-destruction.

Now, there is a challenge confronting the young such as has rarely faced any human generation on earth. There is no time to start from scratch to build a new culture and new values. Not all in the past was hypocrisy. That the young are endowed by the past with the gift to recognize hypocrisy and evil, testifies to this. They must separate the kernels from the chaff.

They must never lose their social awareness and human concern. In order to survive, mankind needs active participation on the part of every one of them. They should realize that if they "drop out" the consequent loss to society is immeasurable. Their radicalism should be measured by their constructive contributions to society. We are running out of time.

The challenge to build a just and better world for us and others and to preserve the existence of our planet and our species—is the only way we can compensate for the innocent death of six million Jews who loved life and followed justice. Our very existence depends on accepting this challenge and on its rapid fulfillment.

Of course, this is a challenge for the immediate heirs of the people directly involved in the Holocaust—the Germans and the Jews. Both must face up to the Holocaust without weeping, and also, without sweeping it under the rug of silence. German youth can compensate for the past by following the way of German redemption as outlined. This is the only way, and nothing less can rid them of their collective guilt. The Jews face the greatest challenge of all. They feel perhaps that they do not owe any compensation, since their people suffered and perished, and they also feel betrayed and forsaken by God. They are wrong.

The essence of being Jewish is to follow justice, which is embodied in Jewish commandments, ethics and morals without regard for personally suffered injustice. If men, in general, propose to compensate for the death of the six million victims by increasing the intensity of personal and collective conscience, Jews, specially, should be compelled to it by the accepted obligations at Sinai (Exodus 24), for which their parents and brothers perished in Auschwitz. How can a Jew, in this world of conformity, mediocrity, and lack of conscience, shrink from such a valiant stand and remain Jewish? The answer is plain: he cannot.

The old Jewish anthropomorphic description of God, though not so physical as in Christianity, might be responsible for the religious crisis of some Jews after the Holocaust. In that sense God could have forsaken the Jews in Auschwitz, as He had forsaken Jesus on the cross (Matthew 27:46): "And about the ninth hour Jesus cried with a loud voice, saying, *Eli, Eli lama sabachtani*, that is, My God, my God, why have thou forsaken me?"

But the Jewish God, in spite of those attributes and names like "Father," "King," "Fighter," has been so presented only by the simple folk who were lacking the philosophical grasp of the Almighty. God cannot be described by any words. He definitely has no human attributes and therefore no human behavior: He doesn't forsake anybody as a human being would. In the daily prayer *Yigdal* we say: "He is inconceivable, He has no form of body, and He is no substance."

If, indeed, we forget the old anthropomorphic God and accept that He is inconceivable, it makes no sense to rebel against Him and to abandon Him because He never left us.

The Jewish people have found their way to God and His commandments in pursuit of righteousness. Righteousness gives a man a feeling of security, psychological balance, and purpose in his existence. In their Covenant on Sinai, Jews accepted God's commandments as the guiding rules of justice. They assumed that the anthropomorphic features of God include divine justice also. If God is inconceivable, this man-given attribute cannot be ascribed to Him, and rebellion against "this God's justice" in Auschwitz is nonsense. In the Holocaust was born the third phase of the evolution of Jewish theology: Man is responsible for his own deeds and God is only the Creator, Who endowed man with free will to make the right choices. The previous two phases were mentioned before: a) rejection of human sacrifices and b) rejection of animal sacrifices.

Jewish theology will have to deprive God of His old attributes. Here, perhaps, is the great role the Holocaust will play with Him in Jewish religion: it will bring man closer to God. One should use human logic and descriptive methods only within the range of the human. This cannot apply to God, Who is beyond that range.

Though the Jewish faith was shaken and biological losses were immense, Jews remained spiritually stronger than others because of the awareness of the preservation of individual conscience and righteousness while the world around them was losing both. Perhaps, because of the suffering and injustice in the ghettos, camps, and forests, Jews subconsciously swore to follow the codes of human justice even more than they had before. They left their old anthropomorphic God, Who they thought had forsaken them, there, and swore to the real One from Mount Sinai, the inconceivable One, the universal God of Job, that they, a people of Jobs, make a New Covenant with Him (before He had made one with them) to follow justice always and to uphold the Covenant of Sinai. And the ram's horn was not there, nor were there flashes of lightning or thunderbolts. Instead, there was the dim glow of the crematoria as a Fata Morgana in the time of the earth being "*tohu va'vohu.*"

Chapter X

A WARNING

The Holocaust was unthinkable only before it happened. Once it occurred, it set a precedent and can be repeated, not necessarily with Jews, but with any powerless group in any society. The only way that it can be prevented is by mass education, enforcement of democratic ideas, and the strengthening of the individual conscience. The young generation is more sensitive to human needs, more ethically motivated than the older generation, and is aspiring toward spiritual growth. It is therefore more likely to free itself of indifference, an abhorrent and dangerous characteristic of the old.

Even if they are agnostics, it might give the young a cool shiver to suggest that if they follow the last seven commandments given on Mount Sinai they will be protected from becoming robots that kill.

No better law has ever been written to secure human rights. Seeking truth and justice unceasingly as a principle of education, to be open-minded and seeking freedom of expression as a basis of communication, avoidance of dogmas and bigotry in interethnic relations, and the desire to build life constructively and help all human beings-these are the protective measures necessary for avoiding another Holocaust. Teachers and psychologists, clergymen and physicians, most any professional and non-professional men who come into contact with others have the opportunity to influence them and to generate in their hearts the warmth of humanitarian ideas till they become a way of life and glow with a fire of brotherly love for all men, a fire stronger than the hell of Auschwitz.

We must realize that methods leading to the goals of social reconstruction have to be based on the same humanitarian precepts as the goals themselves. Each system in the past promised those who supported it an eventual paradise, either here on earth or in heaven, in the meantime causing a daily hell and disaster. That any totalitarian methods are considered good, no matter how morally or ethically ugly they are, and that the same degenerate robots can serve any totalitarian system as long as they know the inhuman methods required by the ruthless government is proven by the two documentary reports from Simon Wiesenthal. In one[1] he named prewar fascists and Nazi collaborators who later united in action with the anti-Jews from the ranks of the Polish Communist party. Their course of action, which they label anti-Zionism, was the same as in East Germany and in Soviet Russia. These prewar fascists, who, during the war, helped the Germans in the extermination of Jews, partially infiltrated the Communist party where they were later attempting to implement a racist approach to socialism. In his second report[2] Wiesenthal named those who worked in the Nazi press and propaganda or were prominent members of the Nazi party and later worked for the German Democratic Republic.

This is a warning to the young who do not realize, in their noble attempts to rectify injustice, that they can become pawns in the vicious game of replacing one brutality with another—their own.

EPILOGUE

What is the lesson to be learned now that the fires of the Holocaust are extinguished? What is the [victi]m's first reaction to this cosmic tragedy? Should the world that let this happen perish, should attempts [be] made within the existing system to change it?

This *"Apres nous le deluge"* attitude is certainly unjust and traditionally unwarranted. There were [plen]ty of innocent victims among other national groups from which the oppressive forces were recruited; [som]e of them saved the Jews at the risk of their own lives. There were also many examples of goodness [and] unselfishness among the populations of occupied Europe during Hitler's regime. The whole Danish [nati]on followed the example of its king and his government in making a strong defense of the Jews and [com]ing to their rescue. Despite enormous pressures, terror and the brutalization of the citizens of the [vari]ous countries, many nuns and priests offered help to the sufferers. In Lvov, Metropolitan Andrew [She]ptycki, head of the Greek Catholic Church in Galicia, hid a great number of Jews in his church and [app]ealed to the Ukrainians to cease slaughtering the innocent. In Vilna the Mother Superior of the [Ben]edictine order supported the Jewish resistance movement. Oscar Schindler, German, saved over a [thou]sand Jews. More than this number of Jews was saved by the Japanese Vice-Consul in Kovno, Sempo [Sug]ihara, who issued them transit visas to the Dutch West Indies, through Japan. These are but a few [nam]es that should be remembered by the survivors of the Holocaust.

How, then, can the victims of Nazi oppression condemn all mankind? They should remember [Abr]aham's argument with God (Genesis 18:23): "Will You indeed sweep away the righteous with the [wic]ked?" No. He will not. All men must join hands with those who recognize the trespasses against justice [and] use their capabilities to prevent the dehumanization of our species.

Francois Mauriac[1] outlined the mission of former Nazi prisoners to teach the world about the catastrophe. Also some of the Jewish survivors were asking themselves: how and why did they survive when so many millions perished. Was it perhaps to bring about a change in human relations and attitude, to erase forever the discrimination and hatred toward their fellow man, and most of all to serve as warning to mankind so that the tragedy of the '40's will not be repeated?

Understanding the gravity of this mission, those of us who had forgotten the word "love" in the ghettos, will start to recite again, twice a day, as they had daily since the Revelation on Sinai,

"And you shall love."

It is high time that our Christian brethren, for whom Jesus should be the highest authority, finally accept His teachings as it is written in Matthew 22:36-40 "Master, which is the great commandment in the law? Jesus said unto him: "Thou shall love the Lord thy God with all thy heart, with all thy soul, and with all thy might. This is the first great commandment. The second is like unto it. You shall love thy neighbor as thyself. On these two commandments hang all the laws and sayings of the prophets."

There were the *Righteous Gentiles* during WWII, who risked and sometimes lost their lives to save or help Jews. They stand out against the black sky of history, like bright stars. How few they were! Even today, in peaceful times, there is so much hatred and prejudice even in this country. Yet others make their voices heard in defending democratic liberties and love for Jews and for Israel, for example, the California Christian Committee for Israel, Bridges for Peace, the International Christian Embassy and Shalom International. They work for nurturing love and not for converting Jews.

I undertook to study the reaction to an historical cataclysm, in general, and to the annihilation of European Jewry during World War II, in particular. How much do people really know about this greatest of human massacres and what impact did it make on their moral attitude? What are their psychological responses to this suffering of cosmic proportions? How do they apply their values-their ethical, philosophical, and religious beliefs-in assessing such an historical event? How would they relate it to the conditions of the present day? What would they propose to prevent a tragic repetition of history on an ever larger scale?

In an attempt to answer some of these questions I conducted a survey along two lines: first, an evaluation of spontaneous opinions expressed by some of those who saw an exhibit of the scenes of the Holocaust, and the second was through the collection of answers to questionnaires.

A traveling exhibit presenting the brutal extermination of innocent men, women, and children by the Nazis was presented in libraries and educational centers on the West Coast, primarily in and around Los Angeles. The Committee on Documentation of the Congress of American Jews from Poland, a historical and philanthropic organization prepared the exhibit. It consisted of enlarged reproductions of captured Nazi photographs, pictures, and relics contributed by the survivors of the concentration camps, together with books and a recording of portions of the Eichmann trial. The objectives of the exhibit were twofold: to acquaint the younger generation with the most tragic and brutal events of all recorded history, and to remind us that these events must not happen again. Viewers of the exhibit were invited to make comments. Five hundred entries were analyzed.

The answers to the questionnaires were obtained from two hundred and three people, considered a representative sample of educated American society on the one hand, and former European Jews, some of them concentration camp inmates, Israelis, and Germans on the other. (See Table 1). The questionnaire is an outgrowth of my meeting with the German Catholic group, *Pax Christi*, in Hamburg, Germany, for whom I prepared the questions ad hoc. While developing the project I retained the same questions for all subjects in this study. The questions were as follows:

    1. What were the underlying reasons for the persecution of the Jews by the Nazis and why were they singled out for annihilation as a nation, race, or group?

    2. How and why did the German people allow this to happen?

    3. Were the Jews in any sense responsible for it? Did they bring it on themselves?

    4. How could Jews of the '40's have avoided or changed the course of action against them?

    5. Could Jews have defended themselves, and how?

    6. Could the Germans have revolted?

    7. Does the guilt of the German people still exist today? Would you subscribe to the idea

"forgive and forget[91]"

8. Is the new German generation responsible for the deeds or rather misdeeds of their fathers?

9. What can I do to compensate for the past—as a German, a Jew, or just a man?

10. Can such events be avoided in the future? What measures could be taken?

11. What is the lesson to be learned by mankind from the past injustices?

TABLE I. PARTICIPANTS RESPONDING TO THE QUESTIONNAIRE

LISTED BY CATEGORY AND OCCUPATION

Totals	American Jews	European Jews	American Gentiles	American Students	Germans	Israeli Students	Occupation
22	8	4	9		1		Housewife
76	5	2		59	2	8	College Student
4			3			1	Nurse
5	1		4				Secretary
13	6	2	5				Medical Doctor
9	2	2	5				School Teacher
16	5	5	6				College Professor
3	2	1					Psychologist
7	4	2	1				Engineer
6	4	2					Clerk
1	1	4					Pharmacist
11	7						Businessman

2	2						Orthopedist
4			4				Nun
2			2				Executive
1			1				Real Estate Broker
2		2					Lawyer
1		1					Veterinarian
1		1					Biologist
1		1					Social Worker
1		1					Newspaperman
1		1					Insurance Agent
10		10					Former Inmate
2		2					Former Partisan
1		1					Banker
1		1					Jeweler
203	47	45	40	59	3	9	

A smaller group of solicited comments on the Nazi atrocities was obtained from several well-known personalities and was treated separately, as not representing "the man on the street." Only in this small group will the participants be revealed.

As expected, the spontaneous remarks of the viewers of the exhibit reflected primarily their emotional reactions to the horror, or their accompanying feelings, while the answers to the questionnaire, though often directed by the emotions expressed knowledge (or lack of it) of certain facts, opinions and the moral stand of the participants. Some answered immediately, some took weeks to prepare. Only a few needed help from others in the formulation of their thoughts. However respondents did find it most hard to answer the questions. Of the many questionnaires distributed in Hamburg, Germany, only two were answered. A friend of mine, who, in spite of long preparation and the promise to answer, did not return the questionnaire, said to me: "It is hard to come close to that period in history. You smell the stench."

Many of the expressed reactions to the Holocaust had to be eliminated to keep the size of this book small enough for the average reader. Numbers in parentheses indicate the same answer given by several viewers. Some of the responses reflected the superficial minds of those who are unable to grasp the gravity of the matter. Others, because of their preconceived opinions, showed a nasty attitude, seeing no reason for raking up the horrors of history.

But the majority of respondents considered this study extremely important. Each of them attempted to come to terms with the subject, as much as possible, without emotional overtones, to find a solution in this challenging, almost intractable area of ethics. They felt that the questions they were asked to answer could not remain rhetorical.

Responses to the exhibit itself ranged from the passionately outraged to the detached and critical. They also uncovered some appallingly depressing anti-Semitism. For the most part, they show that even at a distance of almost thirty years men were still affected deeply by the pain of their fellow men.

For some the horror is perhaps unbearable. For example, there was a dramatic scene at the exhibit at the University of Southern California. One of the viewers fainted. It turned out that he was a Ukrainian who recognized himself in the picture, standing before an oven in the crematorium. Now a worker at the university, he explained that as an inmate he had had to feed the oven with corpses. This response was more meaningful than a written comment.

"Atrocities are horrible, but showing them is much worse".

"The exhibit destroys the peace and composure of the viewer. He wants not to be disturbed in his life of pleasure and complacency."

"Let us stop rehashing history."

"The exhibit repeatedly induces nausea instead of teaching man to love."

"There is sensationalism, shock, disgust, bitterness and anger."

"Where is love in the exhibit?"

Two people in this study saw the anti-Judaism of the Nazis as a bribe of German opinion; twelve, as simple robbery.

"Self-pity and hatred toward men is wrong."

"The exhibit causes fear of right-wing Nazism in America; there is nothing about the left wing."

"The exhibit is commercial and emotional. Sixteen million died for racial reasons, and not only six million Jews."

"The mourning and hatred of the exhibit are inadequate goals."

One man doesn't see the purpose of the exhibit. (2)

"The exhibit seems to show perverse pleasure. "*(4)*

"Too great emotional impact of the exhibit."

"This exhibit doesn't reach the man on the street."

"Lack of pictures of victims of Nazi medical experimentation." (2)

"Too little—too late."

"Pictures cannot reproduce the true horrors."

"It is not necessary to display this because people are aware of what went on in Europe."

"More documents needed."

"Bring the exhibit out to every city in the world."

"Get an exhibit arranged to contact different denominations."

"You should book the exhibit on a temporary basis to any group that is willing to show it."

"Make it into a travelling exhibit." (2)

"The exhibit should include pictures showing the type of care and placement the survivors were given."

"Put English titles on." (2)

"Give additional explanatory notes and sub-titles in English." (4)

"Translation should be interesting."

"Should be permanently displayed." (2)

Several people returning the questionnaire stressed the clash of ideas between Judaism and Nazism. Two of them felt that the Germans feared a strong ideological enemy; two said that the Germans feared a people who knew how to survive. Three recognized the opposition of the state-nation-leader complex to Jewish monotheism; one, the opposition of the design of a chauvinistic society to a cosmopolitan attitude; one, the opposition of dictatorship to Jewish individualism.

"Additional pictures should be on display showing shame, regret, and helplessness of Germans and Poles who wanted to help the Jews."

"We should enlarge it-not only present the Jews of Poland, but also those from other European countries."

A few sounded like voices crying in the wilderness:

"Bertrand Russell—where was he?"

"Exhibits like this are seen by too few, understood by fewer, and disregarded by many."

The pictures precipitated some sideline thoughts.

"Is 'Jew' a race or religion?"

"Read *Europe and the Jew*, by Malcolm Hay- -an insight into present day anti-Semitism."

"How can we build a new Jewish life in the U.S. when Jews are divided?"

"Try to use lights to enable people to feel the gloom of the past."

"Try to use the example of the American Constitution, which guarantees the God's given rights for the individual."

"Should be exhibited downtown—City Hall, Los Angeles." (2)

"Needs more publicity."

"Should point out the forces that brought the Nazis to power."

"Should be shown in many more places." (3)

"Put up a big sign to attract people."

"Should be shown all over the USA." (2)

"Should be shown periodically (perhaps every year)." (5)

"Should be made on a larger scale."

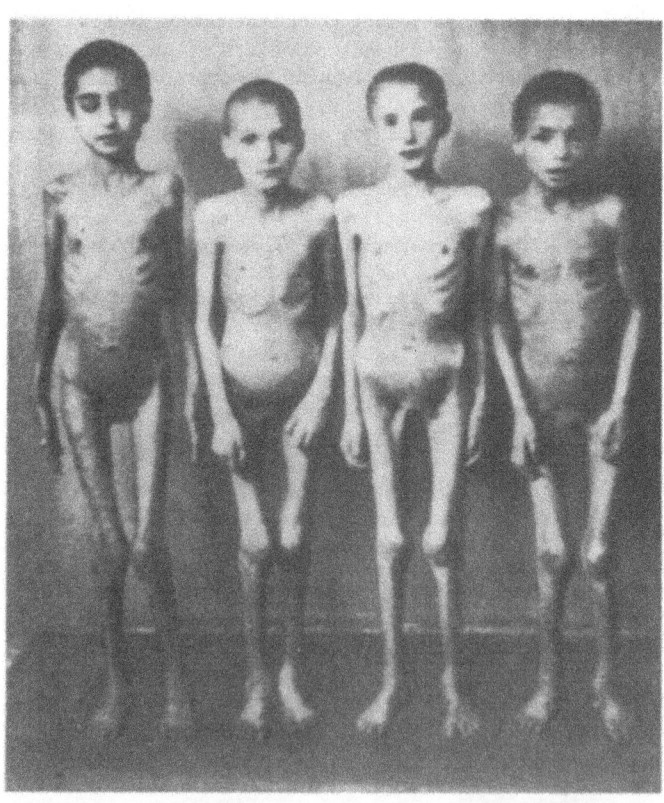

Children in Brzezinka camp. Photograph from the collection of Dr. Mengele, SS camp physician.

"You Jews are lucky, you have your own country, you are free, virile, and happy. Keep it this way."

"Here in America we have a lot to be thankful for."

"Jews have no hope outside Israel. They face only barbarity and violence among their hosts."

"Let all Jews unite and be faithful to each other."

"The British have imprisoned their fascist leader, and Rockwell got killed in the U.S."

"We are far removed in time and space from these horrors."

"College students of today are the adult population of tomorrow. They will accept mature responsibilities in community and family."

"Let us populate Israel before we get caught in the pond of plenty." (2)

"We must return to the land of our forefathers. We must become masters of our own destiny."

Others reacted to the remarks of earlier viewers by making comments of their own:

"There is no need for the perverted expression of humor. This is life and death, liberty or domination- not comic book stuff."

Main gate of base camp at Oświęcim showing inscription in German, "Work Brings Freedom".

"Reactions to the exhibit are very, very interesting."

"Anti-Semitic exclamations are perverted expressions of humor."

"Each people that suffered should display its own exhibit."

"The comments are more terrifying than the exhibit."

We can see, then, that even those who are far removed from the atrocities of the Nazi concentration camps, whether by time or ethical background, reacted personally when our exhibit provoked them. When men are directly confronted with the reality of human suffering their compassion and concern becomes evident. But they must have the horror or the danger visibly before them; it must be experienced. This exhibit reminded men of what has already occurred. It is horrible enough, yet an even greater horror effecting all of mankind permanently may soon befall us. What will it take to make us actively aware of our possible fate? We have much to learn from the past, but we must also apply our lesson to the present, now and quickly, before we find it to be too late.

It has become obvious that a totalitarian regime may easily perpetrate crimes against individuals and groups without fear of resistance. At the same time and more subtly, by the dehumanizing of mass culture, by arresting individual conscience and unleashing the incalculable destructive powers of a sophisticated technological system, it can slowly become the greatest danger to all of mankind. The Nazi Holocaust was exactly this. We must learn from the past in order to avoid an even more drastic historical replay. The rule of totalitarianism is the same, though the victims may vary. The catastrophe that befell the Jews was not just an isolated unfortunate crime of a diabolically inhuman system. It is a portent of what might happen to us all. For men who do not accept the Revelation on Sinai let love be kept deep in their hearts. "Love men or perish."

Two persons answering the questionnaire brought up the idea of the savior. Of these, one maintained that the Nazis were attempting to prove that their party was the savior; the other, that Hitler was the savior.

Four persons in this study believed that the Germans suffered from insanity, an inferiority complex,

A college professor-writer said: "All people in the aggregate are not like sheep, they are sheep. They live on cliches and prefabricated sentiments, and they wait for some energizer and organizer to change them from a passive state to an action state."

A number of participants in the study tried to understand the behavior of the Germans by their direct relationship to the Jews or by basing it on religion. One Baptist engineer arrived at the following conclusion: "Man is born sinful since Adam. Satan has many followers."

Ten wrote that the economic depression in Germany brought about the situation. According to two, Hitler found a solution to the economic depression..

We may no longer say that we learn nothing from history. If together we all are about to start an accelerated effort to protect mankind from the perils of a holocaust, we have to do this, not necessarily free of sin, but definitely aware of our shortcomings and guilt even at the price of an unpleasant catharsis. The effort can be successful only if we are sincere in marching from the fires of Auschwitz to the burning bush of Horeb, from blind instincts of destructiveness to the unbending spirituality and love. The dying morality is crying out for immediate resuscitation.

„Wer gegen den Juden kämpft, ringt mit dem Teufel." Julius Streicher

Julius Streicher and anti-Jewish propaganda

APPENDIX

Here are some answers to the questionnaire and also entries of viewers of the exhibit, who spontaneously addressed their remarks to the unknown to them questions.

The question: How and why did the German people allow this to happen was answered by twenty-two people who saw strong propaganda as the causing force; another twenty-two indicated that the answer was to be found in the influence of Hitler, a madman, a powerful speaker with a charismatic aura; thirteen said that it was the group feeling of a superior race-the *Herrenvolk*, and that a new "Jesus" arose to lead them out of the wilderness.

Eleven felt that nationalistic ambitions, once fired into action, override anything even a race of people; three, that the Germans were in search of national pride and self-esteem; two, that the German society consisted of a nationalistic minority and an apathetic majority; and another saw a murderous minority and a nationalistic majority. This was Darwin's theory applied en masse.

The Germans were ignoring the situation, said eight; they pretended that it did not exist, and they buried their heads in the sand. One sees what one wants to, said five others.

Could the Jews have defended themselves, and how? Eighty-eight people answered simply: "No." One wrote: "There is no real defense against the brutality of humanity. One may kill and be killed, or not kill and still be killed. One must overcome his own fear. People exploit one another's fear-- exploit one another's loves and attachments. People cannot defend themselves from brutal selfish man in any way except to become like him and give kind for kind. In my opinion the Jews were defenseless in Germany."

Another: "Would anyone have believed them if they had foreseen the treatment they would receive from the Nazis?"

Others: "They were not equipped for it psychologically." (2)

"They were pacifists."

"Spread out among other populations, they had an aversion to war."

"No, unless they could have possibly appealed to other governments."

"They had no friends. They lived in a hostile environment." (2)"

"They had no arms."

"They had close family ties, (unwillingness to sacrifice members of the family)."

"Physical defense was impossible."

"No. Neither could other nationals."

"There was no defense possible."

"Doubtful. " (5)

"I don't know." (34)

"Yes. "(10)

"Maybe, by good organization and leadership." (5)

"Maybe by military organization (early enough, perhaps in 1933)." (9)

"Possibly." (15)

"Yes, by mass exodus." (2)

"Yes, by a powerful underground movement." (2)

"As the Jews in Warsaw did." (8)

"Some Jews did defend themselves, and courageously." (3)

"They did defend themselves, also by evasion, resistance to law."

"If Jews of the world had projected their influence on their countries, it might have helped."

"Attempts should have been made on the part of the Jewish community to establish better public relations and arouse world sympathy." (5)

"Yes, by being submissive to the Germans."

"By admitting that this was really happening, by banding together, by abandoning their traditional mold. This probably would not have stopped the injustices, but it would have put a sizable dent in the German Holocaust procedure."

Dear Sister, It is hard to believe and to admit today that this really happened. At that time we were not "on Cloud Nine," not on LSD; we were very much indeed admitting that this was true and not a nightmare.

"Yes, by uniting in a common desire not to submit." (4)

"By fighting or by an earlier Zionist movement."

"I do not know whether they could, but I admire the faith that chooses not to!"

Dear Professor, I appreciate your high esteem for the Jewish faith, but I have to say that there are no precepts whereby a Jew is not permitted to defend himself!

"They could have refused to cooperate with the Nazis for special favors. Many turned their fellow Jews in."

Dear Professor, you are an authority on physics, but, sorry to say, you know nothing about Jewish-German relations in the ghetto. If you should desire to look for historical sources, please do not consider Hannah Arendt's writings as such!

"Only by some miracle such as suddenly growing new foreskins for themselves."

An Israeli: "Yes, by using guts and by unification."

A German: "Had more Jews been prepared to offer themselves as sacrifices in open resistance, world opinion might have been mobilized against Hitler in the early stages."

Eighteen participants in the questionnaire study did not know if the Germans could have revolted. One said: "The Germans should have revolted. People then were no different from what they are now. People do not want to risk being tarnished in the world of politics. For a whole generation to be so lacking in a moral stand is appalling."

Others said: "I oppose revolt. I would have hoped that many Germans would have refused to participate in the persecution of the Jews; but in the light of what such a refusal would have cost, I dare not be self-righteous in condemning individual Germans."

"They could have done so even at the ballot box in 1933."

"I don't understand this question. Which Germans revolted against whom?"

"Revolting is foreign to the German *"Ordnung"* mentality." (2)

"That is like asking a pack of wolves, after killing fresh meat for dinner, to give it to the poor rabbits."

"The individuals could revolt; the mass, no." (2)

"At the first they could have revolted, later, no." (15)

"They probably could." (7)

"Maybe they couldn't." (2)

"They could not." (34); because of the great terror of the Nazis (4); because they were happy with Hitler. (3)

"They could have revolted." (108).

"Some tried" (5).

" They were not interested." (35)

The following indicates what viewers at the exhibit had to say in connection with "Forgive and Forget":

"A Jew who protects free speech for a Nazi, Rockwell (Wirin, a known member of the American Civil Liberties Union) is guilty of promoting Nazi ideology. If we had more such Jews, the history of the annihilation of Jews could be repeated."

"I lost few relatives in the war and don't feel bad about the German people."

"Leave the judgment to historians."

"Let bygones be bygones."

"Forget the atrocities." (2)

"Forgive and show love. Jews received enough sympathy."

"The theme 'lest we not forget' is wrong."

"The war is over."

"Not to forget what?"

"We should forget, because it is a source of embarrassment and shame to Germans, and it is psychological masochism for Jews."

The question of guilt, forgiveness and remembrance was tackled by a number of people.

One woman in this study said: "I seriously doubt that there is much guilt for the German people except as isolated individuals. Few of us want to carry the sins of the past around with us. Few of us care to accept any responsibility for our actions. You might as well forgive and forget. You are not going to revive the 5 or 6 million dead, or take the suffering, which they endured, from them. Nurturing hatred is unhealthy for any group of people although people do usually nurture it. It prevents people from learning about themselves and gives the ideal historical excuse for further hating which only leads to further bloodshed."

Another woman: "I do not believe there is too much guilt. Some feel badly from the viewpoint of the rest of the world. Some individuals may feel sincere regret. But people spend very little time contemplating their sins. It is uncomfortable. I would subscribe to forgiving, but how can one forget? I believe there will be little forgiving and forgetting, people being what and as they are. There will probably be more herd instinct and more deep hatred with a tangible basis to feed it. Such a tragic thing, for those who suffered it and such a sickening thing for those who did it, to have done! Will not one seek revenge and the other self-justification? Has it not always been this way?"

An Israeli writes: "They did it as a nation and therefore the guilt of the nation still exists and will be with respect to years in which the crime was done. As far as present and future relations between the Jewish nation or its political representative, Israel, and the German state are concerned, I believe that they should be measured according to the present situations and interests, which does not mean forgiveness, and we should not forget the past."

One German answered that the guilt of the German people still exists today. Another says: "Every single conscious and responsible individual who lived during the Nazi times cannot feel without guilt.

Twelve people did not know enough in order to answer the questions. Others differentiated guilt as an act from the feeling of culpability, giving only a description of one but not the other.

One asked: "What guilt? The German people are starting that old thing again. History does repeat itself." Another adds: "Did it ever exist?" Still another: "Ask the Germans."

Other voices: "We are all guilty." (2)

"The guilt, I am afraid, lies with more than just Germany.... Other nations let this happen.... This is not the kind of thing one can easily forget. Our responsibility lies in not letting something like this happen again."

A Catholic nun: "Yes, the Germans are still guilty, and all bystanders also. It is not a matter of 'forgive and forget' but rather to teach, to be understood and to learn for both sides."

"Why open the old wounds?"

"Only God can forgive."

"One cannot forgive or forget on behalf of those who are not here anymore to speak." (11)

A Quaker writes: "A non-Jew cannot say 'forgive and forget' concerning a Jewish tragedy of such incredible character. But, in general, I believe in forgiveness as far as it can be genuine."

Still others: "To forgive and forget is a matter of the needs that the Jewish people are going to encounter."

This is a false approach! Forgiveness should be a function of moral justice and not of convenience.

"Do we have a practical alternative?"

"Germans of today should not be considered guilty anymore than Jews of today should be blamed for the death of Jesus."

"No people must be allowed to develop the paranoid Nazi delusions."

"Only individuals can be guilty."

"Everyone makes mistakes; for example, the U.S. in Vietnam."

"With the rise of a neo-Nazi party in Germany I am led to believe that the Germans would do this again."

Twenty-six did not know if the Germans were guilty and seven whether they deserved forgiveness.

"They are possibly guilty." (3)

"They don't feel guilt." (7)

"Few consciously feel guilt." (15)

Eighty-five pronounced the present Germans guilty.

Said one: "Forgive gradually, perhaps in a stretch of a few generations."

"Forgive partially." (2)

"Forgive." (64)

"Don't forgive the guilty individuals." (24)

"Forgive not." (34)

"Forgive and forget." (11)

"Forgive not and forget not." (48)

"Forget." (11)

Seventy-two warned:

"Never forget!"

Unfortunately, hatred and destructive tendencies are not altered in some even as they are directly exposed to exhibits of the Holocaust. For example, here are some of their comments:

"Why is the inflection of horror constantly associated with the one ethnic group, the Jews?"

"The Jews want to invoke sympathy and capitalize on previous suffering" (from an Arab student).

"Nietzsche and Wagner were just as good as the good Jews—Jesus, Freud, Marx, and Einstein."

"The Jews must feed their guilt at least every fifty years to remain above the Gentile world."

"I fail to see what good the exhibit is; it brings only unneeded sympathy for the Jewish race." (3)

"It makes people realize that UCLA has a very militant and dangerous Jewish community".

"Too bad that the Germans did not have more time to finish their work" (from a Rumanian student).

"Get the kikes out of the way in order to take care of the Catholics and Presbyterians. T o d t z u d en J u d e n.

These ten comments show that two per cent of the viewers of the exhibit retained the irrational prejudices we now associate with demented, aberrant Nazism. Their anti-Jewish feelings, though perhaps psychopathological, are still with us and we had better be aware of the fact!

Six people viewing the exhibit expressed criticism of both individuals and nations that maintained their position as "bystanders."

"Crime is committed not only by commission but also by omission."

"The world was silent. This proves its association in the crime."

"The American people were silent. The American government was silent."

"Where was Bertrand Russell? Why was he silent?"

Many sought to express the historical significance of the period in a single sentence or two; others by an exclamation. Thirty-one merely expressed shock and terror:

"Neo-Nazism is a product of a decaying social system."

"This happens when nations follow fanatic leaders blindly."

"Germans, including German Jews, were complacent because of their atheism."

"I am very moved by the plight of Jewish people."

"Nazism was born from the injustice of the Clemenceau policy toward the Germans after World War I."

"Allied nations created the moral vacuum in prewar Germany."

"Nazism is a creeping socialism."

"Nazism is a blot on Western civilization--the result of technology without humanity."

"Nazism is egocentric, destroying itself and the human community at large."

"It is the fate of the Jews to be perpetually destroyed."

"The religious difference of the Jews led to their annihilation."

"Being falsely accused of communist sympathies, the Jews had to pay with their lives."

"The decaying social system is to be blamed for the atrocities. The real enemy is the German as well as the American Nazi."

"The real enemy is the unscrupulous imperialism. International capitalism formed Nazism in order to fight communism indirectly. A similar upsurge can take place again in the U.S." (2)

"Why did the Jews let themselves be slaughtered? The German army did not number six million."

"Let us find the cause of the hatred of Jews that always results in atrocities."

"Jews are always the same; they have been kicked around so long and will be kicked again if they don't shape up."

"If the Nazis hadn't persecuted the Jews they would have won the war."

"The crime was perpetrated by literate, cultured, scientific people."

"Germans negate the truth of killing."

"Dictatorship and the one-party system are very dangerous."(2)

"Dictatorship is a fanatic abomination."

"This was the worst destruction of Jews in history."

"Wake up, America!" (2)

"It is a horrible tragic epic in man's history." (2)

"It is a reminder of tragedy, of horror, of war, and of hatred."

"Let us do research on the basic causes of the greatest catastrophe of the 20th century and possibly of all time."

"Jews were forced to endure inhuman suffering."

"Why do Jews always have to suffer so much?"

"It is unspeakable horror!"

"We need to remember, to become involved, to know what happened."

"My blood boils again."

"It shows the master race triumphant (picture where Nazi soldier beat up a Jew; a truckload of bodies later transformed into soap and lampshades)."

"It is unforgettable." (4)

"I cannot forget."

"I should not forget." (2)

"It is an inferno of agony." (3)

"We shall remember it."

"It is a horror of mass insanity." (2)

"Let us be aware of what happened and let us do something about it."

Twenty-four people associated the Holocaust with past or present events, and with the American scene:

The annihilation of Armenians by the Turks. (2)

The injustice done to Nisei here in America in World War II. (4)

The mistreatment of American POWs by the Japanese.

"See U.S. imperialism in Latin America."

"The American treatment of Indians and Negroes should be shown."

"Remember Khrushchev's handling of the Ukrainians."

"In thirty years from now Germans will show atrocities of the U.S. in Vietnam, and Johnson will be called Hitler."

"People in the U. S. are brainwashed to believe that the Soviet Union is our real enemy."

"We criticize the Germans. What right do we have to do so?"

Twenty-seven viewers of the exhibit tried to offer some psychological evaluation of the Holocaust:

"Nazi crimes are products of hate and indifference."

"Nazi crimes are products of atheistic thinking."

"There, but for faith, go all of us."

"This is a product of cruelty and sadism of the German people."

"A creed based on power and success is an affirmation of a pessimistic view on life."

"The human community is ridden by an awful guilt, and it must accept responsibility for the genocide of the Jews."

"Man has potential barbarian qualities."

"We all are sadists capable of violence and destruction."

"Criminals are neurotics and psychotics."

"The lowest human instincts were responsible for these acts.

"The Germans changed into a brutal mass of people under the leadership of a wicked man."

"The Holocaust is a result of hate and discrimination."

"The exhibit proves man's infinite capacity for evil, his monstrous appetite, and inhuman intelligence."

"This is a lesson of man's greed for power."

"The hatred of the Jews goes much deeper than the hatred of the Negroes."

The philosophical considerations are expressed in the following remarks:

"The son of a man is basically good. Give him a chance to exercise his goodness."

"Some animals call themselves men. Let them live as animals."

"We live in an era of gentile barbarity."

"Christ asked two thousand years ago, 'What is truth?' Is the inhuman slaughter of millions of innocent people truth?"

"Cold-blooded murder cannot be explained by demands of national defense or the duty to follow orders."

"Nazi gas chambers brought the death of a race, and now governments prepare the death of the human species."

"Hatred is the source of all human misery."

"Nothing can bring back the destroyed lives."

"The silence of bystanders was an association in crime."

"What keeps the world tormenting Jews?"

"When does a Jew start being a Jew and when does he stop?"

"It is earth's hell, anti-utopia, sadism, cannibalism."

"Germany did not invent genocide."

"Let us examine our own virtues."

"Man cannot live without history."

"The world has many hungry people who are anxious to seize the hope of God at the cost of democracy and humanity."

"Not just the Jews were wronged by the Nazis, but also the people of the world."

"Jews suffered torture, tyranny, degradation, and lost six million, but now they have a free country. The Armenians suffered under the Turks, and lost three million and don't have their country."

"What could have been done to help those who suffered?"

"Tragedy lies not in the fact that the victims were Jews but that they were human beings."

"Here is the essence of all that is bad in culture."

"Tools like these are the only weapons against the beasts of suppression and torture."

"There is a loss of faith in human values."

"Love thy enemy is God's teaching. We need the love of God in our hearts."

"Have in your heart love for your fellow man." (2)

"Thou shall not kill."

"Let's spread the Christian idea: forgive and forget."

"'Forgive them for they know not what they do,' said Christ."

"Is there that much evil in the world?"

"Man has to change for posterity's sake."

"How can a man have so many inhuman feelings?"

"It makes me doubt the existence of God, although it was this belief in God that caused Jews to be murdered."

"As long as we never forget the past, freedom may come just a little bit sooner."

"How can man have faith? You and I are responsible for all the evil actions."

"Hate and horror are still with us."

"We don't learn from history, because we don't want to."

"How can our living God find forgiveness in his heart to excuse the atrocities?" (2)

"Any life is sacred, regardless of color, creed, or nation." (3)

"Let us show respect for each individual as a child of God."

"Sufferers and those who impose the suffering are human."

"There is need for positive action to forgive and forget. (If one nurtures bitterness, let us not forget that it is a sign of neurosis.)"

"A philosophical whitewash, but not personal forgiveness."

"Grow beyond shock and self-righteous anger through contemplation and positive action."

"No exhibit will change human nature. Let's concentrate only on changing the pattern of human behavior."

"Can we understand the German viewpoint and not be prejudiced against them?"

"Man himself devised the measures and actions against his fellow man."

"The technical performance of evil usually attracts more attention than evil itself."

"Prejudice still exists."

Answering the questionnaire, twenty-six people thought that the Jews had no power and were therefore an easy target. One person felt that some Jews were rich; five, that being economically superior to the Germans, Jews presented a real competition for Hitler; one, that their threat was both real and imaginary; and one, that they had a great influence.

What happened to the Jews was a result of how the Germans felt about them: thirty-four said that Germans were jealous and envious because of Jewish economic superiority; seven thought it was because of economic and mental superiority; thirteen, that the economic jealousy was combined with competition and fear; and two, that this combination was in addition augmented by intellectual anxiety. Two said that Germans were greedy. One student said that the Germans were afraid of the socialism coming from the East and the fact that Lenin was Jewish. A Gentile saw Christian fear of Jewish success. Only three American Gentiles and three European Jews saw the religious or Church--inspired anti-Judaism as the basis for singling out the Jews. A Baptist said that this was God's punishment of the Jews for not following His commandments.

Many Jews and Gentiles, as evident from my questionnaire, are choosing the terms "scapegoat" and "eternal traditional or historical anti-Judaism" as the reasons for the persecution of the Jews by the Nazis. Twenty-six people saw the Jews as scapegoats for the economic conditions in Germany; eleven, for the political situation of the country; sixty-eight, for "general troubles." What befell the Jews resulted from traditional anti-Judaism, according to nineteen and from historical anti-Judaism, according to twelve. One of the latter group felt that this was an historical condemnation of the Jews and their ideology. Eight saw an acute expression of the latent anti-Judaism of the German people. Ten said that all was done to divert German attention from real troubles. One man found fault with the Jews who lost their identity; one, because they had a feeling of superiority; one, because they called themselves "Chosen People;" and one, because they failed to leave Germany while there was still time.

Five people, in their answers, blamed the Germans, saying that the Nazis were themselves convinced that what they did was right; twenty-eight, that the Germans did not want to get involved, were apathetic and were unwilling to take an unpopular stand; twenty-eight others also attached blame to the Germans for a number of related reasons: the "follow the leader" mentality, unquestioning submission to authority, obsessive concern for "law and order," the "robot mentality," and the idea of obedience, in addition to the desire to avoid pain, to gain pleasure, to survive and to enjoy. Said four, the Germans acted under the ancient animal code and belief that all means are good.

Plain robbery was the motive, according to three; two maintained that it was indifference to the persecution of members belonging to another group. Two said it was sadistic perversion, lack of civil courage and failure to understand and defend democracy. Self-centeredness was also mentioned.

Seven people felt that the injustices suffered by Germans after World War I at the hands of the Allies led to what happened; two felt that World War II was responsible, that the Germans would probably have disapproved of these atrocities in peacetime. They showed willingness to blame others but not themselves. One person observed that the silence of the Western Powers played into the hands of Hitler. Fifteen people could not find an answer to the question. One had an indirect answer: "How and why did we allow the recent Biafra slaughter?"

The Ghetto Memorial in Warsaw.

"They are not responsible except when they subscribe to Nazi ideology instead of feeling guilt for their fathers' deeds." (S)

"The shame of the deeds persists. Perhaps this is one of the greatest problems of the young,."

"They should share the feelings of guilt because the events were not individual acts, but perpetrated by a nation against nation."

There were nine answers to the questionnaire that considered the reasons why Jews were singled out, including their being different in external appearance; and nine that had to do with self-imposed separatism and easy identifiability.

"Their heritage was the robberies which enriched present-day Germany."

The responsibility of the Germans for the Holocaust was discussed as follows:

"We all are responsible."

"The present German generation is responsible (9); and so are all bystanders."

"They are responsible: as a historical lesson."

"They are responsible only in that they are children of the proposed 'Master Race'."

"They are responsible in part." (2)

"They are responsible only in so far as they remain unaware, unrepentant, and unwilling to work for a world free of such things."

A German answered: "Indirectly they are responsible. In the German nation today there is a generation gap greater than elsewhere, primarily as far as this problem is concerned and because of it. The young generation opposes the refusal of the older people to admit the responsibility for the crimes. However, the problem is not solved by this stand, since the new generation is also a German one, and the crimes were committed in the German name. The young can try to build up trust with great patience."

A Protestant American writes: "The new German generation is definitely not guilty. I do not want to accept blame for the fact that my forefathers were slave traders or that the slaves were brutally treated. I feel no guilt or responsibility for this. Beyond the desire not to be like them in my attitudes, feelings, and actions, I do not feel I should be 'punished' by Negroes on account of my forefathers."

Fifteen did not know how to answer this question. At the exhibit some commented:

"It (the Holocaust) was a surprise to complacent civilized mankind."

"The new generation of Germans has the feeling of guilt and shame." (2)

"Young Germans don't believe that these atrocities were true."

"Young Germans believe that the Allied Powers erected the ovens and built the electric barbed wire."

The following comments on the exhibit illustrate the power of love as a deterrent to a possible other catastrophe:

"Is it true that it "couldn't happen here? Are we really so very different from the Germans?

They were not barbarians. Their civilization was an example of high culture, producing a Durer, a Goethe, a Beethoven, a Gutenberg and a Luther. The Jews of Germany who attained such eminence, were so integral a part of their culture, that when reflecting on German Jewry we think immediately of a Rothschild and an Einstein. Germany, like America, suffered through an economic depression and established a democratic government. They were vocal for morality, wholehearted in philanthropy, and brave in battle. They were noted for their politeness, industry and initiative. They loved their families and their country, had an active religious life and some of the world's most respected academies of learning. Then almost overnight, the cultured ladies and gentlemen of Germany began methodically murdering their fellow man in a slaughter unparalleled in human history.

"Can all the blame be laid upon a megalomaniac dictator and his small band of gangsters? No. Those gangsters could not have taken even the first step, unless there was something of vital importance missing from their culture."

In analyzing the answers of the participants in this study to the question: Were the Jews in any sense responsible for what happened to them? One can see a definite lack of understanding. Instead of addressing their answers to Jewish responsibility for their own deaths, most tried to answer questions which could be formulated as follows: Was there anything wrong with the Jews that they were not liked? Why in the world did they wait that long among unfriendly people, knowing well that they were going to be killed?

Only one student made it known that he indeed understood the questions. "Yes," he said, "the Jews were responsible for it. By confessing their faith they brought it on themselves. If they had only wanted self-preservation, they could have denied their faith. They knew what they faced and faced the consequences."

This student shows a lack of knowledge of history. Jews could not have bought life by embracing Christianity or Hitlerism. Christians of Jewish descent were also killed.

Another responded: "Who knows? Man clings to an idea, kills for it. He tries to destroy an idea by killing the people who hold that idea. Man hates what is different from him, and what he does not understand, he fears. Man has never risen above the necessity of grouping together for survival, and therefore, grouping together is still a necessity of survival, and sometimes the indirect cause of destruction. Man will not join the human race. He sticks to his own race, prejudice, creed, or cause, and fights."

Fifteen people did not know how to answer. One gave an unqualified "Yes." Most of those who felt that the Jews carried some burden of responsibility tried to explain in what way; so often the accusation was so mild that it did not only exonerate the Jews but ironically denied any such possibility. Some answers:

"The victim of any bully's attack brings it on himself by merely existing. The culpability of the victim lies only in being available." (4)

"They hid their heads in the sand."

"They failed to see the reality of the threat."

"They believed, 'This cannot happen here'. " (6)

"They believed that the threat of the Nazis would only be directed against the eastern, non-assimilated

Jews."

"Maybe by being too meek and submitting passively; by being defenseless." (5)

"Yes, by blind submission to the Germans."

"Only in the sense that they maintained their group identity." (2)

"Yes, they were 'more German than the Germans.' They considered assimilation as insurance: by being German first and Jewish second." (7)

"Yes, just by being Jewish."

"Yes, because of assimilation."

"Those individual Jews who supported the Nazis or otherwise trafficked with them, or who, being ashamed of their Jewishness, helped to confirm in the minds of others the anti-Semites' contention about the Jews, were guilty."

"Some individuals, perhaps. All Jews are judged by the deeds of each and every one of us." (2)

"Jews brought envy upon themselves through the riches of a few like Rothschild and the other money-lenders, and through cultural and scientific leadership." (2)

"Perhaps in opposing the sort of Nordic supremacy that Hitler advanced, yet the reason for this opposition was the fear of the consequences of that policy—fears that were well founded."

"They hated this dictatorship and therefore stood in Hitler's way."

"The Jews had accepted the fact that Christian society did not like or accept them as social beings. They (Jews) had accepted the guilt of Christ's death as their responsibility. With this mantle of guilt and social leprosy they had lived in their own groups and settings through the years. Those that saw what was coming took their money and left the continent. They expected to be persecuted. I can't say that they were unwise, because what they expected came to pass. There is a smell that draws the predator."

One wrote: "By being a separate group, by different traditions, by adherence to special group beliefs we may be said to bring things on ourselves. Even so, there is the Christian idea of the universal Jew: worldly, selfish, un-Christ-like, loud, conniving, whatever...which prevents any other group from fully accepting him as simply an individual human being...but rather as a Jew...a certain type of person who bears watching. Many Christians even in America are wary of Jews and feel that any attempt to be a Christian is stupid. There is a great misunderstanding and contempt among them. The Jews in their history have also persecuted other people when they had the power and the authority, and most people feel they will again."

There are many Christians who repeat this inherited song *ad nauseam* instead of trying to learn facts. Indeed, they close their eyes and ears and refuse to learn. They will get part of the answer from this book, if they can stand to read it, and part from Bertrand Russell's: *I Am Not Christian*.

Two people felt that the Jews were responsible because they were perhaps too arrogant and too important for a minority group; six, because they were clannish "separatists."
"All human beings are responsible for the human conditions."

This last is a very interesting concept, which *ipso facto* makes the innocent victim responsible for his own murder.

"They did not resist in the mass, as they should have done." (2)
"They should have tried to go underground and to resist." (3)
"I see no Jewish responsibility though I do see a tragic complicity on their part in that they- -as a powerful or at least united group- -did not act sooner and with strength against the fascist genocide. I think this was due to the sudden and vicious force of said genocide."
Ninety-five persons answered simply: "No."
"Nonsense."
"No one can bring such crimes upon himself."
One said: "The Jews respect the rights of each individual as a human being, whereas the non-Jews think in terms of being subservient to a dominant personality.'[1] A former concentration camp inmate-said: "No! Self-accusation is the worst answer. Any possible Jewish weakness cannot and should not serve as an excuse.[91]

A Protestant professor of religion and an author wrote: "The conspicuous faith and life-style of the

Jews made them a natural target. But, thank God that the Jews have been willing to pay the price for being different. In this sense it is sad that more Christians also did not bring the same persecution on themselves: the Jews should feel complimented." One German student answered, "How?" The second said," Officially guilty,' they made it lighter for the government to divert attention from real life. Two Americans also gave the same answer.

"Jews showed lack of solidarity and organization," (5) was a further comment of interest and calls for some elaboration.

That which was missing was a deep conviction of the equal value of each human life, and a genuine commitment to the community of man. Without this conviction and this commitment, the door is open to hatred, suspicion, fear, arrogance, cruelty, cynicism, prejudice and every form of human depravity. We needed to remember this at the time of this study, when our country was defining its moral role, when we have witnessed the brutal murder of our youngest president, when social and political extremism was on the rise and fellow Americans were battling for their basic civil rights.

One wrote: "It is so easy to shut our eyes and ears to our neighbor's problems, to be generous with our words and frugal with our deeds. From three major American cities recently, came news of helpless people murdered in the full sight of passive onlookers. When asked why they did not help or even telephone for the police, they were reported as saying. 'We did not want to get involved.' We need an exhibit such as this to shock us out of our complacency; to remind us what happens when we do not actively engage in the fight for right.

We are our brother's keeper! His civil rights are our civil rights; his happiness and safety, our happiness and safety; his social progress is our social progress. This exhibit brings home to us painfully, that this is not just an abstract of religion or a question of philosophical morality, but the empiric of civilization's survival."

The prominent actor and musician Steve Allen wrote: "This exhibit clearly shows what happens to a society that becomes 200-per cent patriotic, smug, intolerant, and prejudiced.

Education alone is not the answer, for the Germans were a well-educated people. Religion alone is not the answer, for the Germans were a religious people. And democracy alone is not the answer, for Hitler was endorsed by the overwhelming majority of Germans. What is needed is emphasis on the importance of love. The world must never be permitted to forget this example of what happens when a nation hates better than it loves."

Chancellor Franklin D. Murphy of the University of California at Los Angeles said:

"The period of the Nazi atrocities inflicted on the Jews of Europe is surely one of the blackest examples of what has been called 'man's inhumanity to man.' This unprecedented perversion was carried out on such a vast scale that it is almost impossible for many to comprehend that such premeditated evil could have in fact occurred, especially in the twentieth century and on the continent from which much of Western civilization has developed. I suppose many would prefer to acquire an amnesia about this epoch, for certainly all civilized members of world society must feel a little personal guilt that this could have happened in our time. Yet, because it did in fact happen in our time, we must never be allowed to forget it. The memory of this evil episode in human history must serve to sharpen our conditioned reflexes so that we are prepared to spring immediately and vigorously to the defense of civil liberties and human dignity when and if other bigots or psychopaths begin to show their true colors."

Senator Thomas Kuchel: "Civilized peoples of the world must never be allowed to forget or become calloused to the almost inconceivable and fiendish inhumanity which resulted in extermination of uncounted victims of Nazi depravity.

Regrettably, it is a natural trait as memories dim for successive generations to believe that shameful incidents of the past are unlikely to be repeated. This is a hope to be nourished but history has demonstrated that the conscience of mankind requires repeated reminders if true progress is to be achieved.

The supreme sacrifice by millions of innocents beastly tortured and slaughtered in a shameful drama of horror must be indelibly etched in the minds of all civilized beings as a safeguard against revival of prejudice, hatred, and intolerance which put a reprehensible stain on the annals of the Twentieth Century. "

Senator Kenneth Keating wrote: "I feel that you have undertaken a project of utmost importance, for it is well established that those who forget history are compelled to relive it. By acquainting our younger generation with these tragic events and reminding ourselves, we are insuring that this will not happen again."

Senator Stuart Symington said: "We should make every effort to see that all men who live, as well as those who follow, will never forget the brutal acts of inhumanity which were inflicted upon the Jewish people during the Second World War.

For it is from a full comprehension of such acts that we can gain an unyielding determination to remain. vigilant to the task of assuring every individual in our society, regardless of race, color or creed, the protection of just laws imposed by just men. Without such a determination, the delicate balance between the interests of the state and the individual is placed in jeopardy."

Let us now see what advice people a generation later can give the inhabitants of the ghetto. Twenty-six could not take a stand, but most thought they knew the answer:
"By having a stronger Jewish identity." (3)
" By settling in Palestine." (2)
"By overcoming the alienation from the Germans through social assimilation." (2)
"By becoming ardent supporters of the Reich."
"By being more alert and active in revealing the real truth in the field of propaganda."
"By more widespread reporting of what was being done to them."
Further comments: Two thought that the Jews could have spoken up and taken action:
"By a coordinated and unified public relations program."
"Perhaps by sacrificing all material possessions and leaving immediately."

"They might have rallied behind their underground and supported more openly the fighting against the Germans, rather than labeling them trouble-makers."

"They could have refused to cooperate with the Nazis for special favors. Many turned their fellow Jews in." (2)

"They have since developed a strong will to survive and through standing up for their rights have just recently matured."

"They stood up not only for their own rights but also for the rights of other people long before the birth of many nations—this is what makes them Jews."

Others said changes could have been brought about: "By doing what their country, is doing today- stand and fight."

"By becoming as militant as the British."

"By massive revolt." (10)

"Jewry abroad, especially in the United States, should have exerted more pressure on their respective governments." (10)

Forty people felt that the Jews could not have changed the course of events at all.

"No one could have changed the course of action at that time as the Jews did against their enemies in antiquity. Very few Jews were willing to die for the good of their group."

"The Jews could not achieve anything effectively because the military government of Germany was anti-Semitic."

"No Jews in this world could have helped to avoid the course of history, as all the civilized people in the world had been waiting for these happenings." (2)

"Only with the help of an outside intervention, both by active support and change of the immigration policy, could they hope to change their fate." (7)

Is any compensation for the past possible? If there is, what can one do? The opinions of the present generation are of great interest.

Twelve people in the questionnaire study said flatly: "Nothing." Eighteen said: "No compensation for 6 million lives is possible." Three felt that it is impossible for the Germans to compensate—for the most part these express the opinion of the majority.

Some other opinions are: "One does not compensate for the past; one learns from it to correct social injustices of today in order to build a better future." (6)

"I feel no necessity to compensate for something that was neither of my design, within my power to prevent at any level, nor even within my age." (3) "'Compensation' or 'reparation' in the sense of striving to untangle a can of worms which is the past is a fallacious and fruitless concept. Every man's obligation is, regardless of how the situation came about, to serve present need, seek present justice and avert present threats."

An Israeli: "In an American any feelings toward compensation would stem from compassion, not from guilt."

A German: "Know the past. Work for the present and the future. There is a need for a generally organized action opposing neo-fascism, when necessary by use of force." A black student added: "To admit and to tell others that America and the rest of the world are racist and that racism is bad must be the policy."

Thirty-four participants in the questionnaire study believed that such events could be avoided in the future by education about the atrocities and fanaticism of the past, early recognition of such events by the mass media, and immediate counteraction.

Examples of other comments on avoidance were: "Support international dialogue and cooperation, especially economic." (3)

"The UN, given real power in the form of a strong peace-keeping force, could play a major role in helping to avoid such events. Concerted effort of the entire world could prevent the recurrence of such events before it develops further." (6)" By avoiding being brain-washed by flag-waving and manipulation. Your individual conscience and ideas of right and wrong have to take precedence over orders." (5)

"Only socialism, not nationalism, will bring a solution."

"Yes, by returning to God's good Grace by recognizing and accepting His Son as a personal Savior."

"Disarmament is the only answer."

"Yes. Israel strong and powerful enough is the answer. She will accept any Jew any time." (4)

"The fading out of religious differences and pretensions will be of great help. Abundant intermarriage of the Jews with the gentile population would greatly enrich the quality of human beings in all parts of the world." (2)

"Definitely yes. It is of paramount importance to preserve the state of Israel. In time of peril the existence of Israel would lend moral and diplomatic support to the Jews in the Diaspora. It would also spur our incentive to stick together. Give us the dignity which we lacked in previous years and recognize the fact that a Jew is a Jew, no matter where he came from or where he now lives." (3)

"Perhaps. One should provide an economic safeguard for all and initiate broad attacks on social problems." (8)

"Such events are part of the human sickness. Only the change of man's nature could avoid them." (4)

"No. Propaganda is stronger than education."

"No. Look at the world's passivity in the case of Biafra."

"No! Anti-Semitism is here to stay." (2)

"No, except never to be passive again, as the Jews were,

not knowing or believing what was occurring." Twelve did not find an answer to the question.

The viewers of the exhibit commented: "It can happen again."

"It can and will happen again." (2)

Is there a lesson to be had by mankind from past injustices? The most challenging aspect of the interhuman relations-tolerance of other members of one's own species, if not love, is not always reflected in the answers to this question in this study:

" There is none."

"Man never learns."

"Unfortunately mankind has not learned a damned thing yet! Consider Hungary, Czechoslovakia, Korea, Biafra, Cuba and on and on. (4)

"The lesson is the one Christ tried unsuccessfully to teach men."

Thirty-one people could not answer this question.

"Man's nature is a fight between good and evil."

"We should love the image of God in each other."

"We are people, human beings, all of one blood."

"We must remain free."

"Man is basically good. Give him a chance to exercise his goodness."

NOTES

Chapter 1

[1] Jack Miles : God , A Biography, Vintage Books, and New York 1996.

[2] John Cairns : Matters of Life and Death : Perspectives on Public Health, Molecular Biology, Cancer, and the Prospects for the Human Race. Princeton University Press, 1997)

[3] Andrei Sakharov : Progress, Coexistence and Intelectual Freedom, W.W. Norton and Company, Inc., 1968.

⁴A. Powell Davies, The Meaning of the Dead Sea Scrolls, New York: The New American Library, 1959

⁵ B. Dagobert D. Runes, The Jew and the Cross, New York: Philosophical Library Inc., 1965.

⁶ Edward H. Flannery, The Anguish of the Jews, New York: The Macmillan Company, 1964.

⁷ Trophim Kichko, Judaism Without Embellishment, (Ukrainian) Yudaism bez Prikras, Kiev, 1963.

⁸ Chrysostom, Adversus Judaeos, Homilies against the Jews (in French translation: Joannou Cou Krusostomon, ta Eurixkomena Panta, Oeuvres completes de Saint Jean Chrysostome, ed. J. Bareille), Paris: Louis Kires, 1865.

⁹ Jules Isaac, The Teaching of Contempt, New York: Holt, Rinehard, Winston, 1964.

¹⁰ Carl J. Friedrich and Zbignew K. Brzezinski, Totalitarian Dictatorship and Autocracy, New York: Frederick A. Praeger, 1964.

¹¹ Hannah Arendt, The Burden of Our Time, London: Secker and Warburg, 1951.

¹² Peter Pulzer, The Rise of Political Anti-Semitism in Germany and Austria, New York: John Wiley & Son, Inc., 1964.

¹³ Raul Hilberg, The Destruction of the European Jews, London: W. H. Allen, 1961.

¹⁴ Martin Luther, About the Jews and Their Lies, (German) Von den Juden und ihren Lugen, Luthers Werke, Weimarer Ausgabe, 53 Bd., 1920.

Chapter II

¹ Hannah Arendt, op. cit.

² Ibid.,

³ Trials of War Criminals before the Nuremberg Military Tribunals, Washington, D.C.: U.S. Government Printing Office, Vol. XIII, p. 127.

⁴ Ibid.

⁵ Ibid., p. 125.

⁶ Ibid., p. 127.

⁷ Ibid., pp. 318-327.

Chapter III

[1] Erich Fromm, Escape from Freedom, New York: Avon Books, 1966.

[2] Fromm, op. cit.

[3] Ibid.

[4] Otmar Freiherr von Verschuer, Rassenbiologie der Juden, Forschungen zur Judenfrage, Vol. III, Hamburg, 1943.

[5] Der Giftpilz, Verlag "Der Sturmer", Nuremberg, 1938.

[6] Friedrich Burgdörfer, Die Juden in Deutschland und in der Welt, Forschungen zur Judenfrage, Vol. III, Hamburg, 1943.

[7] Helmut Schramm, Der Judische Ritualmord. Eine historische Untersuchung, Berlin, 1943.

[8] Heinrich von Treitschke, Deutsche Geschichte, New York ANS Press, 1915-1919.

[9] Martin Luther, op. cit., pp. 524-526.

[10] Hermann Rauschning, Hitler Speaks, London, T. Butter-worth, 1940.

[11] Norman Cohn, The Myth of the Jewish World Conspiracy. A Case Study in Collective Psychopathology, Commentary (June, 1966).

[12] Hilberg, op. cit.

[13] Forschungen zur Judenfrage, Hamburg: Hanseatische Verlagsanstalt, 1943.

[14] Erich Botzenhart, "Der politische Aufstieg des Judentums von der Emanizipation bis zur Revolution von 1848," Forschungen zur Judenfrage, Vol. III, Hamburg, 1943.

[15] Botzenhart, op. cit.

[16] Kleo Pleyer, "Das Judentum in der kapitalistischen Wirtschaft," Forschungen zur Judenfrage, Vol. II; Hamburg, 1943.

[17] Werner Sombart, Die Juden und das Wirtschaftsleben, 1st edition, 1911.

[18] Sombart, op. cit.

[19] Bolko Freiherr von Richthofen, "Judentum und bolschewistische Kulturpolitik," Forschungen zur

Judenfrage, Vol. VIII, Hamburg, 1943.

[20] Friedrich Burgdorfer, "Die Juden in Deutschland und in der Welt. Ein statistischer Beitrag zur biologischen, beruflichen, und sozialen Struktur des Judentums in Deutschland," Forschungen zur Judenfrage, Vol. III, Hamburg, 1943.

[21] World Medical Association, quoted by Alexander Mitscherlich, M.D. and Fred Mielke in Doctors of Infamy, The Story of the Nazi Medical Crimes, New York, 1949.

[22] Ibid.

[23] Elie A. Cohen, Human Behavior in the Concentration Camp, New York: The University Library, Grosset and Dunlap, 1959.

[24] Gideon Hausner, Justice in Jerusalem, New York: Harper and Row, 1966.

[25] G.M. Gilbert, The Psychology of Dictatorship, New York, 1950.

[26] Elie A. Cohen, op. cit.

Chapter IV

[1] A.Ruppin, Soziologie der Juden, Berlin, 1930.

[2] Wilhelm Ziegler, "Walther Rathenau," Forschungen zur Judenfrage, Vol. II, Hamburg, 1943.

[3] Ziegler, op. cit.

[4] William L. Shirer, The Rise and Fall of the Third Reich, New York: Simon and Schuster, 1960.

[5] Ziegler, op. cit.

[6] Gideon Hausner, op. cit.

[7] William L. Shirer, op. cit.

[8] Hannah Arendt, Eichmann in Jerusalem, New York: The Viking Press, 1963.

[9] Hausner, op. cit.

[10] Quoted by Leo Alexander, "War Crimes and Their Motivation," Journal of Criminal Law and Criminology, XXXIX (Sept. - Oct., 1948).

[11] Flannery, op. cit.

[12] Nathan Eck, "Historical Research or Slander?" Yad Vashem Studies, Vol. VI, Jerusalem, 1967.

Chapter V

[1] Bruno Blau, Das Ausnahmerecht fuer die Juden in Deutschland, 2nd ed., Dusseldorf, 1954.

[2] Hannah Arendt, Eichmann in Jerusalem, New York: The Viking Press, 1965

[3] Document 271, Documents on German Foreign Policy 1918-1945, Vol. IV, Washington, D.C., 1951.

[4] Ibid., Vol. V.

[5] Moshe Kahanowitz, "Why No Separate Jewish Partisan Movement Was Established During World War II," Yad Vashem Studies, Vol. I, Jerusalem, 1957.

[6] International Military Tribunal, Vol. VII.

Chapter VI

[1] Aryeh L. Kubovy, "Criminal State vs. Moral Society," Yad Vashem, Bulletin No. 13, Jerusalem, 1963.

[2] Ibid.

[3] Emmanuel Ringelblum, Notes from the Warsaw Ghetto, New York: McGraw-Hill Book Company, 1958.

[4] Hilberg, op. cit.

[5] Joshua Perle, Diary. See "The Destruction of Warsaw," in Albert Nirenstein, *A Tower from the Enemy*, New York: TheOrion Press, 1959.

[6] Ibid.

[7] Yuri Suhl, They Fought Back. The Story of Jewish Resistance in Nazi Europe, New York: Crown Publishers, Inc., 1967.

[8] Kubovy, op. cit.

[9] Yad Vashem, Jerusalem, 1965.

[10] Congressional Record - Senate, April 18, 1963.

[11] Congressional Record - Senate, April 23, 1963.

[12] Congressional Record - April 18, 1963.

[13] Letter to Dr. Sherman Z. Zaks, American Congress of Polish Jews, June 5, 1963.

[14] Statement issued when the present mayor of New York was in Congress, 1963.

[15] Letter to Dr. Sherman Z. Zaks, April 15, 1963.

[16] Letter to Dr. Sherman Z. Zaks, April 30, 1963.

Chapter VII

[1] Shirer, op. cit.

[2] Though it has been reported and generally accepted that Rommel was forced to commit suicide by taking poison, the method of Rommel's death has not yet been established beyond doubt. The late Charles Howard, who as a legal officer of the military government located in Stuttgart, Germany participated in the interrogation of Keitel, told me that Keitel refused to tell how Rommel died. It is not beyond possibility that Rommel was strangled. Keitel asked that his incomplete testimony not be published. He did not want future German children to get the impression that Rommel had been disloyal and not to spoil the tradition of heroism of the German generals.

Chapter VIII

[1] Rolf Hochhuth, The Deputy, New York: Grove Press, 1964.

[2] Encyclica, "Populorum Progressio", Recklinghausen: Paulus Verl., 1967.

[3] Heinrich Spemann, Die Christen und das Volk der Juden, Munich: Kosel, 1966.

[4] Gisela Wiese, Erziehung zum Frieden durch Versohnung, Welttag des Friedens, 4 January 1970, Freiburg.

Chapter IX

[1] Quoted by John G. Hubbell, "Grechko: Master of the Soviet Military Colossus," Reader's Digest ((October, 1970).

Chapter X

[1] Simon Wiesenthal, Anti-Jewish Agitation in Poland, Bonn: Rolf Vogel,

[2] Simon Wiesenthal, Die gleiche Sprache: Erst fur Hitler—jetzt fur Ulbricht, Bonn: Rol Vogel,

[3] G. M. Gilbert, "The Mentality of SS Murderous Robots," Yad Vashem Studies V, Jerusalem, 1963.

[4] Ibid.

Epilogue

[1] Francois Mauriac, in the Preface to Micheline Maurel, Un Camp tres Ordinaire, Paris, 1957

[1] From descriptive material by Eric Ray, art director of University of Judaism, written for The Exhibition of the Nazi Holocaust.

[2] From a letter by Steve Allen to Dr. Sherman Z. Zaks, American Congress of Polish Jews, May 8, 1963.

[3] From a letter to Dr. Sherman Z. Zaks, April 25, 1963.

[4] From a letter to Dr. Sherman Z. Zaks, April 24, 1963.

[5] From a letter to Dr. Sherman Z. Zaks, April 16, 1963.

[6] From a statement dated April 29, 1963.

The publisher apologizes for any printing imperfections.